Presidential Profiles:

An Intimate Collection of Portraits and Documents

By Jack Behrens and Ben Benson

Oneida County Historical Society
Utica, NY
2003

Table of Contents

Foreword . . . . *by author, historian Robert Ferrell* 5

George Washington . . . . *1st President, two terms, 1789-1797* 6

John Adams . . . . *2nd President, 1797-1801* 8

Thomas Jefferson . . . . *3rd President, two terms, 1801-1809* 10

James Madison . . . . *4th President, two terms, 1809-1817* 12

James Monroe . . . . *5th President, two terms, 1817-1825* 14

John Quincy Adams . . . . *6th President, 1825-1829* 16

Andrew Jackson . . . . *7th President, two terms, 1829-1837* 18

Martin Van Buren . . . . *8th President, 1837-1841* 20

William Henry Harrison . . . . *9th President, 1841* 22

John Tyler . . . . *10th President, 1841-1845* 24

James K. Polk . . . . *11th President, 1845-1849* 26

Zachary Taylor . . . . *12th President, 1849-1850* 28

Millard Fillmore . . . . *13th President, 1850-1853* 30

Franklin Pierce . . . . *14th President, 1853-1857* 32

James Buchanan . . . . *15th President, 1857-1861* 34

Abraham Lincoln . . . . *16th President, two terms, 1861-1865* 36

Andrew Johnson . . . . *17th President, 1865-1869* 38

Ulysses S. Grant . . . . *18th President, two terms, 1869-1877* 40

Rutherford B. Hayes . . . . *19th President, 1877-1881* 42

James Garfield . . . . *20th President, 1881* 44

Chester Arthur . . . . *21st President, 1881-1885* 46

Grover Cleveland . . . . *22nd President, 1885-1889* 48

Benjamin Harrison . . . . *23rd President, 1889-1893* 50

Grover Cleveland . . . . *24th President, 1893-1897* 48

William McKinley . . . . *25th President, 1897-1901* 52

Theodore Roosevelt . . . . *26th President, two terms, 1901-1909* 54

William Howard Taft . . . . *27th President, 1909-1913* 56

Woodrow Wilson . . . . *28th President, two terms, 1913-1921* 58

Warren G. Harding . . . . *29th President, 1921-1923* 60

Calvin Coolidge . . . . *30th President, two terms, 1923-1929* 62

Herbert Hoover . . . . *31th President, 1929-1933* 64

Franklin D. Roosevelt . . . . *32th President, four terms, 1933-1945* 66

Harry Truman . . . . *33rd President, two terms, 1945-1953* 68

Dwight Eisenhower . . . . *34th President, two terms, 1953-1961* 70

John F. Kennedy . . . . *35th President, 1961-1963* 72

Lyndon B. Johnson . . . . *36th President, two terms, 1963-1969* 74

Richard Nixon . . . . *37th President, two terms, 1969-1974* 76

Gerald R. Ford . . . . *38th President, 1974-1977* 80

Jimmy Carter . . . . *39th President, 1977-1981* 82

Ronald Reagan . . . . *40th President, two terms, 1981-1989* 84

George H. Bush . . . . *41st President, 1989-1993* 86

Bill Clinton . . . . *42nd President, two terms, 1993-2001* 88

George W. Bush . . . . *43rd President, 2001-* 90

Ben Benson . . . . *Artist & Collector* 92

Jack Behrens . . . . *Author & Editor* 93

Presidential Profiles Bibliography 94

Oneida County Historical Society 95

Presidential portraits were the work of Ben Benson and were prepared with wax pencils,
layering and a wax base to give each a three-dimensional appearance.

Library of Congress Catalog Card Number: 2003111509
Main entry under title:
An Intimate Collection of Portraits and Documents

ISBN 0-9668178-7-7

Foreword

The distinguished portraitist and collector whose work is the centerpiece of this volume is surely worthy of celebration, quite apart from his achievements in drawing the presidents and his extraordinary ability in collecting historical documents. He has worked for many years, and the result is here in this book --- not all certainly --- but a representative share. It is hardly necessary to relate the importance of presidents in the nation's history and, for that matter, for the history of the world in the century past and that in which we now live. At the outset, the country was so small; estimates of a population of three million during the era of independence did not do justice to the expanse of land, reaching the Appalachians and beyond, that they sought to claim. The population, however, until well into the nineteenth century was so small that Europeans, if they thought about the United States, considered the American nation not worth much time in their international calculations.

But then this era came to an end with the presidency of James Monroe, for he was the last president to wear knee britches. After him came the figures of the rest of the century, notably Abraham Lincoln, for whom the Parliament of Great Britain felt something close to disdain when he took office in 1861. Yet his memory among Britons of all classes was anguish upon his assassination. When the shocking news reached Parliament, the members were stunned.

By the end of the century the British government found itself defied by President Grover Cleveland, who was offended by an effort by the British to extend their territory from British Guiana into a country Cleveland announced was protected by the Great Doctrine of 1823.

In the next century, all now a part of twentieth century history, Theodore Roosevelt assuredly gained respectful attention and then Woodrow Wilson, who proposed a basis for resolving the issues of the World War of 1914-1918, became invincible. Wilson, of course, had intervened with two million US troops and helped the allies crush the German army. The story moves clearly on from there with Franklin D. Roosevelt and Harry. S. Truman addressing the major problems of Europe and the world in 1941 to 1945. The so-called Cold War, which lasted into the 1990s, marked the dueling of the two superpowers, the United States and the Union of Soviet Socialist Republics. Not to mention the marked change in presidential importance during the White House term of George W. Bush. It was a landmark change necessary, I believe, because the United States had to act as a force for order in what has been a dismayingly chaotic world scene.

Ben Benson has drawn most of these faces of our world's history ... and he has done it so well, too.

As his friends know, he is a collector of Americana, in particular manuscripts or signed documents. He has a knack for finding them in lists by dealers that often do not appraise properly the value of items put up for sale. He has specialized in finding these documents which someone with a lesser eye for value would miss. And it, of course, is not monetary value that attracts him, but historical importance. Without the evidence of what important citizens of the Republic have accomplished, their bare actions do not have much meaning. They are, to use the phrase of William Allen White in a book of 1928, masks in a pageant. Ben Benson's collection breathes life in unfolding history of this country.

The history of the American nation consists of a panoply of public figures and holders of offices that now reaches back to a time when no one could have imagined the country as such a huge, powerful and complex entity.

We can now see the history of the past two hundred and fifty years of nationhood. And that remarkable past appears in every page of this remarkable book.

-- Robert H. Ferrell
Ann Arbor, MI
September, 2003

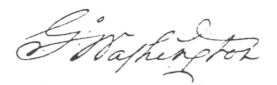

The envelope from Dolley Madison written in her handwriting to Martha Washington was very typical of the vivacious wife of the country's fourth president, James Madison. Said Margaret Bayard Smith, a chronicler of early Washington social scene, Dolley "looked a Queen ... It would be absolutely impossible for any one to behave with more perfect propriety than she did."

Dolley (the surname she chose), a lively, buxom young lady was a clear contrast to her husband, James, who was 43 at their marriage. It was her second marriage ... his first. The contrasts were quite visible. Dolley, who grew up in the strict discipline of the Society of Friends, loved loud colors in her clothing and attire; James preferred black. Mrs. Madison also enjoyed life. Contemporaries reported that she ate heartily and gambled at cards on occasion. She also loved calling on those who had visited her. This envelope, addressed to Martha Washington, could easily have been used to respond to such an occasion. She also enjoyed leaving her card, a poem or even a flower as a souvenir of a visit. It may have been impulse but she did it so frequently, it was believed to be an enjoyable symbol of her nature as a person.

Martha and Dolley had much in common. Both had been previously married and both Washington and Madison had not. Both Presidents, meanwhile, had wed spouses considered fashionable and stylish who were excellent hostesses at the many formal and informal events that were demanded of heads of state. The two women were 26 at their weddings and both had children by previous husbands. The Washingtons and the Madisons were childless during their marriages, however, Martha and her first husband, Daniel Park Custis, a wealthy landowner, had two youngsters, John "Jack" Park Custis, and a daughter, Martha "Patsy" Custis. George Washington adopted them and raised them as his own. Dolley and her first husband, John Todd Jr., had a son, Payne. Although James Madison was patient with Dolley's son, the young man not only mishandled his own affairs, he later mismanaged Madison's estate.

George Washington, while well known as the "father of the country," could have easily had another appellation, "father of US intelligence," too, says author Rod Paschall. During the Revolutionary War, it was Washington's diligence to find and cultivate average citizens like John Honeyman, an Irish-born weaver who became a cattleman, that brought successful results while his demoralized army suffered losses to the powerful British regulars and Hessian troops. Honeyman used his position to travel and do business between American and British lines. A few days before Christmas, 1776, it was a clandestine meeting at Washington's headquarters between the cattle dealer and the general that offered the colonials a risky but necessary opportunity. Washington dismissed everyone from the room and

Paschall believes the general heard enough to plan an attack no one expected at the Christmas season. It led Washington to launch a treacherous Delaware River crossing with his 2,400 soldiers and surprise and rout a 1,400 man Hessian garrison at Trenton, NJ.

The American victory, Paschall contends, demonstrated "intelligence was the major factor in turning the tide for the Americans."

Although he had given years in the service of his country as a military officer, Washington felt compelled to return to public life after the war to salvage the country from continued political chaos. He was elected the first president and then re-elected to a second term. He was the only president to ever receive a unanimous electoral college vote. George Washington died Dec. 14, 1799 at 67.

-- From the Presidential Documents Collection of Ben Benson

Dolly Madison - Envelope written by her to Martha Washington.

John Adams

2nd President 1797-1801

A teacher who wasn't satisfied as a schoolmaster, John Adams used his Harvard education to apprentice himself to distinguished barrister James Putnam to practice law in Boston. As a 35-year-old lawyer, he handled routine personal disputes like the one shown on these pages and, at the same time, stirred controversy among colleagues and foes when he joined co-counsel Josiah Quincy to defend British soldiers accused of murdering innocent citizens in the famous Boston Massacre. Vigorously arguing for clients he would later condemn, Adams won his case to the dismay of patriot editors and his neighbors. Yet, he was popular enough to become the Boston representative in the legislature (General Court). But the issues of liberty and British rule weighed heavily and, a year later, he left public life to travel and relax at the mineral springs of Stafford, CT.

Just 16 months later, Adams re-emerged counseling and writing for popular political papers of the time. His patriotism was so strident that, after he was elected to the Governor's Council, he was dumped by the governor for his zealousness. He loudly supported Bostonians when the waters along the Boston harbor front became fermented from the imported delicacy tossed overboard from moored ships in the famous Boston Tea Party of 1773. A year later, he was a delegate to the First Continental Congress. At 41, he worked feverishly for the appointment of George Washington as commander in chief of colonial forces and for Congress to separate from Britain. He helped write the resolutions that declared America independent and rose to defend the Declaration of Independence at every turn in Congress.

His nervous impatience which served him well during the war years was an unpopular trait when he was appointed to a diplomatic position to help conduct peace negotiations with Great Britain. His patriotic passion irritated the French and worse, he infuriated America's senior diplomat, Benjamin Franklin. He reluctantly recognized his limitations and withdrew to the Netherlands where he obtained American independence and negotiated both a loan and a treaty.

He served in Washington's first cabinet as vice president and entered the presidency at 62. He desperately wanted to end partisan politics, he said in his inaugural address, but a world that continued in turmoil and a cabinet of holdovers from the Washington Administration who demonstrated their disloyalty to the president in the final months of his term of office actually forced him to step down four years later, embittered at Alexander Hamilton and the Federalists.

But he regained the sense of humor that had been with him at times in his career. He became president of the Massachusetts Society of Arts and Sciences among other groups and spent his final days writing erudite, witty, yet petty and crusty letters to his friends.

Adams died on July 4th, 1826.

-- From the Presidential Documents Collection of Ben Benson

President John Adams legal writ in his own hand, written as a young lawyer.

He was called "the man of the people" but he was, without a doubt, the wordsmith of a young nation.

Thomas Jefferson, lawyer, planter, legislator and president, was first and last a powerful writer of world-shaking documents and volumes of personal correspondence that shaped friendships and dueled with opponents.

A patriot, although he angered General George Washington and others during the dark days of the American Revolution when he returned to his Monticello home while the colonial army neared collapse, he suffered humiliation when as governor of Virginia from 1779 to 1881 he had to watch the British invade his state. His friends thought of him as vigorous and tactful but a private man devoted to republicanism ... and family. His privacy about his religious views together with his continued declaration of the need for separation of church and state brought condemnation from New England clergy in the presidential campaign. He was called an atheist and a candidate of the anti-Christ. Jefferson said he believed in God and was Unitarian but he rarely said so.

His Declaration of Independence continues to instill thoughts and dreams of freedom everywhere more than two centuries after it was written.

What is frequently forgotten was his authorship of the Bill for Establishing Religious Freedom, which was adopted in 1786, and the Bill for the More General Diffusion of Knowledge, which wasn't approved. His purpose was to remove artificial or inherited privilege and replace it with the natural mobility of talent and virtue in a free society. His writings were consistent with his life; a general distrust of power and a continued faith in basic law.

His eight years as president were similar to a number in American history; successful the first term but a firestorm of personal and political frustrations in the second.

Jefferson could have sympathized with George W. Bush about an election cliffhanger. His victory wasn't known for weeks because his vote total accidentally tied with his running mate, Aaron Burr, although he defeated his opponent, John Adams. The election results were submitted to the House of Representatives under the provisions of the original electoral college and, while a number of ballots produced no winner, enough abstained to permit Jefferson to finally be chosen president.

Although he was privately concerned about the constitutionality of such a purchase, Jefferson simply couldn't deny the potential for the acquisition of the vast Bayou country of Louisiana in the purchase of 1803 from France.

He remained the "Sage Of Monticello" during the last 17 years of his life spending his time personally directing his farms and mills on the grounds and keeping meticulous charts of the temperature. Death came at 83 on the Fourth of July, 1826, hours before his predecessor, John Adams died. It was an important date in American history, too. It was the 50th anniversary of the Declaration of Independence.

Still a politician seeking ways to help people, he urged the legislation and the charter of the University of Virginia in1819 and was a founder who got the campus located in his own county, planned its buildings ... and served as its first rector.

Yet, said author Dumas Malone in his book, "Jefferson and His Time", while the third president was rich in honors, friendships and achievements such as selling his outstanding collection of books to launch the Library of Congress, "Jefferson had long been troubled by debt, and the failure of a friend whose note he had endorsed brought him to virtual bankruptcy."

-- From the Presidential Documents Collection of Ben Benson

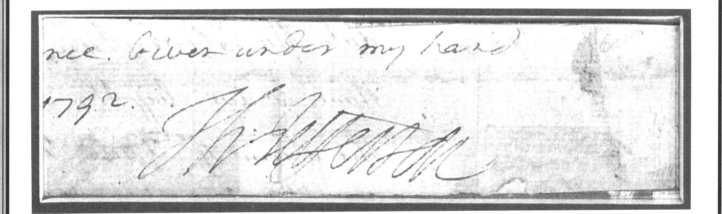

James Madison

A sick and frail man throughout his life, James Madison, the fourth President of the United States, died June 28, 1836, at breakfast while talking with his niece. His valet said death came quickly, like extinguishing a candle.

In his final year, he had painfully watched as Mexican General Santa Anna's 4,000 man army swept over the adobe walls of the tiny San Antonio mission called The Alamo and killed an entire garrison of Texans and Americans.

Yet this nervous and shy wisp of man was the youngest member of the Continental Congress (29) in 1780 and had lived a full life much like his predecessors John Adams and close friend and ally, Thomas Jefferson. Adams died at 91 after only one term in office while Jefferson, who served two terms like Madison, succumbed at 83. Although doctors urged Madison to take medicines so he could live to July 4 (Adams and Jefferson both died on the Fourth of July), the President refused. His death came at 85.

His slight stature (picture 6'2" robust and muscular George Washington standing beside 5' 4", 100 pound Madison) made his lifespan quite precarious in a day when early deaths were commonplace. His physical condition frequently took its toll on his work, too. While he obsessed with trying to restore his health, he suffered what doctors of the time called "bilious fever." It would leave him bedridden and drained of energy for weeks. Contemporary historians believe that Madison's illnesses were brought on by what are called "anxiety attacks" today. Such fatiguing incidents coupled with epileptic fits would have slowed the pace of a much stronger person; not Madison.

A delegate to the Constitutional Convention in 1787, Madison argued strenuously for a strong but limited central government. He wrote sections of the US Constitution and, along with John Jay and Alexander Hamilton, spent hours and days preparing the Federalists Papers to explain the governing philosophy of this young republic. His worst attack came in the summer of 1813 (heat and humidity were usually oppressive in the nation's capital), a year before the British stormed Washington and ransacked the White House. It was Madison's worst nightmare. While he had been warned that capitol defenses were vulnerable, the general in charge assured him that invaders could be repelled. They weren't. Stories surfaced of his wife Dolley Madison's courageous efforts to save White House artifacts and the Declaration of Independence. Wild tales told of the President fleeing Washington when, in fact, he stayed dangerously close to the bombing and pillaging. But public criticism followed him in his final days in office.

   The letter from Albany, NY Mayor Erasmus Corning and the Resolution from the Albany (NY) City Council to Mrs. Dolley Madison less than a week after the President's death were typical of the condolences of a grateful nation to a man who gave so much for the country he loved.

-- From the Presidential Documents Collection of Ben Benson

In Common Council
Albany July 4 1836

His Honor the Mayor offered the following preamble and resolutions which were unanimously adopted

The Common Council of the city of Albany entertaining the most profound respect for the public services and private character of the late distinguished citizen James Madison ex President of the United States do
Resolve. That in the death of this truly great man, his country has to mourn the loss of one of its most illustrious Patriots who achieved our Independance, and of an eminent Statesman who wisely administered the government they had framed.

Resolved. That in conformity to the Resolution of Congress lately passed. the members of this Board will wear the usual Badge of Mourning for thirty days. and recommend to the Inhabitants of this city to adopt the same evidence of respect for the memory of the Deceased. The following additional resolution was also adopted.
Resolved. That his Honor the Mayor transmit a Copy of the foregoing to the Widow of the deceased and express to her the Condolence of the Citizens of this City
A Copy from the minutes.

P. Carmichael
Clerk

Condolence letter written by City Council, Albany, N.Y. dated July 4th.

James Madison   Secretary of State.

5th President 1817-1825 two terms

Handsome and charming, James Monroe disarmed strangers and even enemies with a warm smile and a cordial ease. He grew so popular during his first term in the White House as a Democrat/Republican, the Federalist Party didn't challenge him for a second term.

He didn't have the intellect of a Thomas Jefferson, his mentor, or James Madison, his friend. Nor did he possess a dynamic speaking voice. In a day when there was no Rudy Vallee megaphone or public address system, he was barely audible in a room of a few dozen, some said. His strengths, many felt, were patience and a pragmatic mind to process difficult issues and make wise decisions during his tenure as president. Said a Virginia socialite at one of his final Washington receptions in 1825: "He is tall and well formed. His dress plain and in the old style ... His manner was quiet and dignified. From the frank, honest expression of his eye .. I think he well deserves the encomium passed upon him by the great Jefferson, who said, 'Monroe was so honest that if you turned his soul inside out there would not be a spot on it.'"

He's not remembered by many for getting Spain to cede Florida to the United States and cancel its $5 million debt but those who have taken American history courses have heard or read about the famous Monroe Doctrine. That decree, while not really new, was actually the work of his world-traveled Secretary of State, John Quincy Adams. The Monroe Doctrine became the cornerstone in foreign policy matters for years. It furthered Monroe's own mantra, too; America for Americans.

Yet, his beautiful but very formal wife, Elizabeth, the daughter of a British Army captain, introduced a French custom to the White House that raised eyebrows and ruffled some. Mrs. Monroe ended the Dolley Madison tradition of trading social calls with visitors. Following the French trend, Elizabeth announced she would not receive White House visitors.

Although considered a very private and aloof person, Monroe's wife could be persuasive. While her husband was the US Minister to France, Elizabeth brought about the release of Madame de Lafayette, confined in a French prison and threatened with execution during the Reign of Terror brought on by the French Revolution. The year after he left the White House, he became a regent at the University of Virginia with his friends Jefferson and Madison. Monroe's final six years were spent working on his autobiography. His death, July 4, 1831, at 73 left his final literary work unfinished.

-- From the Presidential Documents Collection of Ben Benson

Mr Monroe wishes to lay, the pleasure to see Mr Gou at ~~the~~ his house this evening, at as early an hour as may be convenient to him.

Sunday, march 8.
Mr Gall

Jas. Monroe
Mar. 8. 1812

Letter written as Secretary of State.

6th President 1825-1829

His qualifications for office were impeccable; 20 years as a diplomat with European countries, 8 years as secretary of state, a workaholic who started at 5 a.m. and usually finished around midnight and, of course, you can't overlook the fact his father John was the country's 2nd president.

John Q. Adams may have appeared the most likely person to succeed, however, his gruff style, arrogance and unpleasantness along with public opposition made his campaign for the presidency most difficult. In fact, Andrew Jackson won the electoral votes. Fortunately for Adams, Speaker of the House Henry Clay, a southerner with his own agenda, supported Adams and gave him the victory ... and received the office of Secretary of State in return.

But it was really a victory for the moment. The precocious Adams, who was thought to be one of America's most learned men, had little to show for his four years other than the opening of the Erie Canal months after he was sworn in and the first Mardi Gras in New Orleans a year later.

He was mindful of his growing opposition from his first day in office.

"Fellow-citizens, you are acquainted with the peculiar circumstances of the recent election, which have resulted in affording me the opportunity of addressing you at this time ... Less possessed of your confidence in advance than any of my predecessors, I am deeply conscious of the prospect that I shall stand more and often in need of your indulgence," he admitted to the country in his inaugural address, March 4, 1825. Stern, shrill and certainly vain, John Quincy Adams couldn't tolerate inferiors. His contempt for his successor Andrew Jackson carried over to inaugural day 1829 when he refused to attend the ceremony. It was the same decision his father had made when he snubbed Thomas Jefferson's inaugural 30 years earlier.

Punctual, religious -- he read the Bible daily -- and starkly Puritan in dress (black), he did have certain quirks which set him aside from the citizen on the street. For example, the President liked to swim nude and one day, when his clothes were stolen, he had to plead with a passerby to go to the White House to get him new duds.

More embarrassing and titillating was his famous encounter with newspaperwoman Ann Royall who sat on his clothing while he took a bath. She refused to budge until he answered her questions in a very unusual news conference.

John Quincy Adams served in Congress nine times after leaving the White House. After his second stroke on the House floor, he was carried to the Speaker's room. He died two days later, Feb. 23, 1848, at 81.

-- From the Presidential Documents Collection of Ben Benson

Given under my Hand at WASHINGTON this Twenty first day of March in the Year of our Lord One Thousand Eight Hundred & Twenty Six and in the fiftieth Year of the Independence of the United States.

J. Q. Adams

7th President, 1829-1837, *two terms*

He was called "Old Hickory," after his favorite jug of home brew from his native South Carolina, and "King Andrew" by his political enemies but President Andrew Jackson was clearly a popular commoner, comfortable with frontier people, farmers, factory workers and hard-working, everyday Americans. John Quincy Adams spoke for aristocratic easterners and some foreign diplomats when he called Jackson "a barbarian who could scarely spell his own name."

The dinner invitation in January, 1833, on this page came as he entered his second term in the White House and was typical for its brevity and awkwardness. He didn't like the social protocol required of those who occupied the mansion at 1600 Pennsylvania Avenue. Yet, Ben Benson's research shows that Jackson in this case, filled out the invitation himself, not a secretary as was usual at the capital. He was a war hero, an Indian fighter, a proud man who dueled three times and once took a bullet near his heart and remained standing to take aim and kill his opponent. His oath of office, March 4, 1829, shocked genteel Washington, DC society when his band of roughhouse supporters followed him back to the White House where they did about as much damage as the British forces had done 15 years earlier. In their exuberance, they broke dishes, ripped down draperies, trampled furniture and carpets and forced the president to flee ... to spare the building of more structural damage. White House staffers wisely moved the big punch bowls out on the lawn and the party continued without the president. Jackson, who had to marry his wife, Rachel, twice because of the scandal that erupted over her questionable divorce from a Kentuckian, lost her to illness days before he became the 7th president. Jackson died at 78 in 1845.

-- From the Presidential Documents Collection of Ben Benson

Navy

The **PRESIDENT,**

Requests the honor of

W. Claytons

Company at   dinner

Thursday the 16th inst at 5 oclock

The favor of an Answer is desired

Rare. Dinner invitation written in hand of President Jackson.
Usually done by a secretary.

M. Van Buren

Old Kinderhook, as he was called, Martin Van Buren was the first New Yorker elected president and, ironically, the first native born American since his predecessors were born prior to the war with the British.

A successful lawyer, the Supreme Court papers (shown here) to recover debt owed the state were typical of his legal work as his Dutch family moved from farming in the Hudson Valley to owning a tavern. It was the latter enterprise that put Martin in touch with powerful politicians like Aaron Burr and Alexander Hamilton who regularly visited his father's inn. In a long inaugural address at the start of his presidency in 1837, Van Buren painted the birth of a new era of good times and prosperity. His remarks hinted at change. "Unlike all who have preceded me, the Revolution that gave us existence as one people was achieved at the period of my birth; and whilst I contemplate with grateful reverence that memorable event, I feel that I belong to a later age and that I may not expect my countrymen to weigh my actions with the same kind of partial hand."

Three months later, his popularity plummeted in the beginning of the Financial Panic of 1837, which began when several New York City banks stopped honoring paper money with gold. The move created a chain reaction of failures among more than a 1,000 banks. It shut down construction projects, financed by the banks, which terminated thousands of jobs. Food riots erupted at the same time. For a cautious and careful politician like Van Buren it was a four-year battle that destroyed his presidency. An amiable man who learned the art of compromise on the bar stools of his father's tavern, it was his unusual relationship with President Andrew Jackson that historians think triggered much of his difficulties. Jackson's well-known personal vendetta with Second Bank President Nicholas Biddle is considered a contributing factor. The economic uncertainty lasted five years and cost Van Buren re-election. His relationship with Jackson demonstrates how political opposites could attract one another. Van Buren, unlike Jackson, enjoyed the theatre, opera, fine wines, foods and expensive wardrobes. He was considered by peers to be a dandy. Frontiersman Davy Crockett once observed Van Buren was "as opposite to General Jackson as dung is to a diamond."

Yet he wasn't a social gadfly either. He was a cautious flirt who carefully avoided the appearance of anything amorous. His wife, Hannah, was a childhood sweetheart. Their 13 year union produced four sons. Hannah died of TB when his New York political career was rising.

While Van Buren said his wife was "unassuming," he intrigued scholars and historians later when he made no mention of her in his 800 page autobiography. He died July 24, 1862, at 80.

Wm H Harrison

9th President, 1841

Some could blame Washington's nasty spring weather. Others might put the blame on the vicious politics of the era.

Certainly fate brought a retired war hero to Washington DC from his modest but comfortable log cabin in North Bend, OH where he was earning extra retirement income as a county clerk to serve his country again at 66 years old.

But popular general William Henry Harrison accepted the Whig Party candidacy to battle aristocratic Martin VanBuren and the Democrats in the 1840 presidential campaign that featured the alliterative slogan Madison Avenue would have loved, "Tippecanoe and Tyler, Too." Little did anyone realize in 1840 that the country would swear in two presidents, not one, a year later.

Ironically, Harrison delivered the longest inaugural address in the nation's history --- an hour and 40 minutes --- on March 4, 1841. Sometime during the proceeding he caught cold which became pneumonia three weeks later and the president was dead of complications a month to the day he took office, April 4, 1841.

While not a party leader, historians said, Harrison's humanity made him a man the country believed would blunt the financial depression his predecessor, Martin Van Buren, handed him. It was also hoped he could end the rancor of partisan politics of the time. People who knew him believed he was considerate, personally charming and generous. Yet, critics said, his generosity would have mired him in more difficulties. For example, he promised cabinet appointments to many and would have been unable to fulfill his commitments.

Said his wife Anna upon hearing of the election results making her husband the 9th president: "I wish that my husband's friends had left him where he is, happy and contented in retirement."

--- From the Presidential Documents Collection of Ben Benson

Written as Adjuant to: General Wayne Anthony.

GEN: WILLIAM H[...]

Born at Berkley, Vir[...]

Inaugurated President of the[...]

DIED APRIL 4TH 1841, AG[...]

The melancholy occasio[...]

APRIL 1[...]

10th President, 1841-1845

Protocol doesn't always create smooth transitions even when prescribed. Sometimes people are left out of the process ... and the last to know.

Sunrise, April 5, 1841, was an example.

Vice President John Tyler was at his home in Virginia where he had been since the inauguration of President William Henry Harrison a month earlier. Tyler's duties, most felt, were simply ceremonial. No one, therefore, had bothered to tell him the president had become ill days after he took office. No one thought to inform him when the president's condition worsened.

Thus, the urgent, loud knocks on his door that morning startled him. The messenger's news was a shock; the president was dead. To his credit, John Tyler made transportation history when he arrived in Washington 21 hours later covering the 230 mile trip by horse, boat and rail from his home in Williamsburg.

His tenure was as stormy as the times. His party, the Whigs, abandoned him and his cabinet secretaries resigned except for Daniel Webster. He promptly replaced them and he refused to be considered an "acting president" even though he had to endure the ignominious appellation, "His Accidency."

Tyler faced congressional wrath as he vetoed more bills than mercurial Andrew Jackson did during his term. Months after he took office the House charged him with impeachment for rejecting a protective tariff act. He forced Congress to pass separate bills. In a short period of time, he made history, too. He was the first vice president to succeed a sitting president and the first to give a second inaugural address the same year. His personal life was much the same. After discreetly mourning the death of his first wife of 29 years, Letitia, who died the second year of his presidency, Tyler secretly married a second wife, Julie, 30 years his junior, two years later while he was still in the White House. Tyler, who died January 18, 1862, at 72, didn't pursue northern politics again when his term ended. He had never lost an election after serving five years in the Virginia State Legislature, four years in the US House of Representatives, nine years in the US Senate and two years as governor of the state. As the North and South separated over slavery and prepared for war, Tyler, a slave owner who had retired to his 1,200 acre plantation near Richmond, supported the southern cause and won his final political campaign ... a seat in the Confederate House of Representatives. He died before the legislative body met.

-- From the Presidential Documents Collection of Ben Benson

his warrant.

John Tyler –

Washington, 23 April 1841

This letter must be submitted to the Secretary of the Navy
J. Tyler

Historians considered him one of the "near great" presidents yet the year before he was elected using a slogan not easily understood --- "Fifty-four Forty or Fight--- few knew James K. Polk outside of Tennessee, his home state. Though he had served one term as Speaker of the House thanks to his mentor President Andrew Jackson and as governor of Tennessee, a boring personality had limited his political opportunities. But that changed in June, 1844, when Democrats at their convention seized a manifest destiny campaign offered by Polk. "I have no hesitation in declaring that I am in favor of the immediate annexation of Texas to the territory and government of the United States. Let Texas be annexed and the authority and laws of the United States be established and maintained within her limits, as also in the Oregon territory," he told the New York Tribune. And, he added, he wanted California, too.

During his four years, Polk risked war with Britain to gain control of half of Oregon and fought a war with Mexico and acquired more than 500,000 miles of territory that later became the states of California, Nevada, Arizona, New Mexico, Colorado and Utah. His policies brought strong reactions. Said the representative from Illinois, Abraham Lincoln: Polk's explanation for the Mexican attack on Americans along the border were the "half-insane mumbling of a fever-dream." He was "a bewildered, confounded and miserably perplexed man," Lincoln said just a decade before he would lead the nation into the worst civil strife of its history. Polk's qualities for presidency were redeeming. Friends and enemies saw him as honest, shrewd and a workaholic who also had another strength; he believed it was the president's job to fulfill the will of the majority ... and Americans saw expansion as important.

A teetotaler among a hard-drinking crowd, Sam Houston once observed about the president, he "drank too much water." And Polk didn't like the socializing or long reception lines that went with the job even if his wife, Sarah, was considered an excellent conversationalist. Card playing and alcohol were banned at the White House during his tenure and even music was prohibited on Sundays. He invented a special handshake to save his fingers during such ordeals. "When I saw a strong man approaching, I generally took advantage of him by being quicker than he was and seizing him by the tip of his fingers, giving him a hearty shake, and thus preventing him from getting a full grip upon me." Polk made it clear he would only serve one term and his work habits and health showed that he virtually predicted his destiny. He died June 15, 1849, just three months after leaving office, at 54.

--- From the Presidential Documents Collection of Ben Benson

I feel great pleasure in being made the organ of presenting to your personal acquaintance Mr. Findley Patterson, of this State, the present Speaker of the House of Representatives at Harrisburg, and long experienced in the legislation and politics of Pennsylvania.

Mr. Patterson is the grandson of one of our oldest democrats of Westmoreland County, Wm Findley, whom I knew well in early life and still remember with great respect. I am sure that I do no more than justice to his merits and standing when I request for him your kind attention and regard.

With sincere respect, I have the honor to be.

Yr. friend and Servant,

G. M. Dallas.

9. April 1845.

His Excellency
James K. Polk
President of U. States.

Scarce: Hand-written letter from Vice-President G. M. Dallas to President James Polk,
The City of Dallas, Texas was named after him.

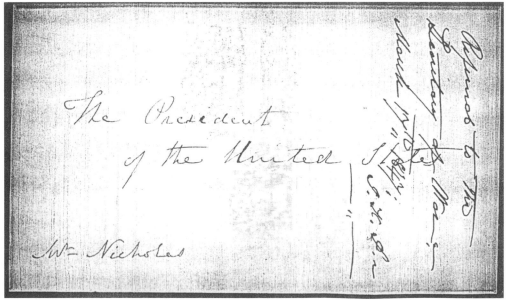

President James Polk envelope addressed as President.

12th President 1849-1850

He considered himself a man of the people and he proved it by spending most of his life -- 40 years --- in the military at distant outposts. Yet he was a wily, stubborn, self-made and a deceptive person. He loved to let people believe his shabby garb --- usually ill-fitting trousers and coats --- made him appear a country bumpkin. Not true, said those who dealt with him. Like Washington, Jackson and Harrison, he was a war hero whose celebrity status gave him political chips. Though he had no formal education and had never voted before, he ran for the presidency and adopted the Whig Party at the same time. His wife, Peggy, may not have been so supportive but she remained loyal. Six pregnancies and the harsh life of the frontier for several decades left her frail and in ill health. She rarely left the family quarters of the White House during their short tenure. But Whig political pros didn't know much about the general's thoughts on governing. They got a quick glimpse on Inaugural Day, March 4, 1849. Taylor made it clear Polk's manifest destiny days were ended. He told the audience in Washington: "In all disputes between conflicting governments it is our interest not less than our duty to remain strictly neutral, while our geographical position, the genius of our institutions and our people, the advancing spirit of civilization of peaceful and friendly relations with all other powers. It is hoped that no international question can now arise which a government confident in its own strength and resolved to protect its own just rights may not settle by wise negotiation; and it eminently becomes a government like our own, founded on the morality and intelligence of its citizens and upheld by their affections, to exhaust evey resort of honorable diplomacy before appealing to arms. In the conduct of our foreign relations, I shall conform to these views, as I believe them essential to the best interests and the true honor of the country." It's always reassuring to hear a general turned president with battlefield victories talk about war as a last resort. He was a 19th century Colin Powell. Taylor, a slaveholder, surprised his party and others when he opposed the extension of slavery into the newly acquired Mexican territories.

It was a typical hot and humid July 4th along the Potomac when Taylor was attending one of the ceremonies to raise funds through contribution documents like the one shown on this page. He returned to the White House to have ice water, chilled milk and a bowl of cherries and other fruit. But Washingtonians had been warned not to eat such things because of a cholera outbreak. The president suffered a bad night and his condition worsened by morning. Diagnosed with some kind of cholera, he predicted he would be dead in 48 hours. He was right. July 9, 1850, Zachary Taylor died at 66. Suspicion continued for more than a century that the president might have been poisoned. His remains were exhumed in 1991 and samples of hair and fingernail tissue were given the latest forensic tests. Experts found no evidence to change the original death certificate.

-- From the Presidential Documents Collection of Ben Benson

President Zachary Taylor. Portion of full document signed as President-contribution to the George Washington Memorial.

Millard Fillmore [signature]

If health care for elderly presidents wasn't a consideration prior to 1840 it became something to think about by 1850.

Both William Henry Harrison and Zachary Taylor, two rugged ex-generals, died in the early days of their presidencies. And both had virtual unknown vice presidents as successors.

Millard Fillmore, called the "forgotten" president, became president in 1850 with the sudden death of Taylor and, according to contemporary historians, was probably better known as chairman of the House of Representatives powerful Ways and Means Committee which dealt with tariff rates in the mid-1840s than any national issues. What was perhaps more embarrassing to party regulars; President Taylor and his running mate were placed on the ticket without meeting.

They met for the first time after the election. Yet, as the stationery and envelopes on this page attest, Fillmore dutifully sent mourning notes and envelopes for six months after President Taylor's death.

The second New Yorker to enter the White House, Fillmore was born in Cayuga County in the heart of the Finger Lakes of a poor farm family. He faced the same dilemma that John Tyler endured; replacing a popular war hero as president. The situation gave editorial cartoonists and writers ample material. Fillmore's speaking style used ordinary words and short sentences and was slow. He wasn't of the caliber of a William Jennings Bryan, Henry Clay, Stephen Douglas, Daniel Webster or others.

Yet, credit Fillmore with vision in foreign trade. It was the 13th president who befriended Commodore Matthew C. Perry and persuaded him to undertake a Far East expedition. His visit to Japan led to opening trade relations between the two countries later in the decade. President James Buchanan benefited from Fillmore's vision and signed an agreement with Japan in 1860.

Fillmore's wife Abigail also played a significant role during her husband's presidency. She was appalled upon entering the 1600 Pennsylvania Avenue residence to find no book shelve ... and no books. An avid reader, she had shelve built on the second floor in the Oval Room and Congress, at her urging, gave her the modest sum of $2,000 to purchase the White House's first library. Millard Fillmore died March 8, 1874, at 74.

-- From the Presidential Documents Collection of Ben Benson

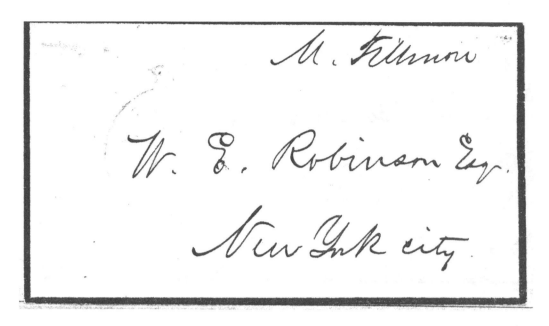

Scarce: Mourning Envelope, Signed and franked by President Millard Fillmore. Dated August 27, 1850. Mourning stationary was used by Fillmore for six (6) months after death of President Taylor.

By the Prefident

It seemed very unlikely that a young (48) New England country lawyer and one-time congressman would offer the compromisan needed to attract slave-holding southerners and win the Democratic Convention in 1852 ... and the national election. But he did.

Franklin Pierce, handsome and charming from Hillsborough, New Hampshire, won the presidency defeating another Whig military offi-cer, Gen. Winfield Scott. Pierce's inaugural address March 4, 1853, offered a good reason, though, as the slavery issue in the border territory of Kansas intensified: "I believe that involuntary servitude, as it exists in different states of this Confederacy is recognized by the Constitution. I believe that it stands like any other admitted right, and that the States where it exists are entitled to efficient remedies to endorse the constitutional provisions."

The new president's stance enraged northerners, encouraged southerners but offered Americans no solutions to a growing political/social/economic issue. Pierce privately was against slavery ... but he lacked the will and determination to seek solutions.

Tragedy struck Franklin and his wife, Jane, days before the inauguration. In a train acci-dent in which the couple was unhurt when their car tumbled down an embankment, their 11-year-old son, Bennie, was killed. Both Franklin and Jane were traumatized for months. Mrs. Pierce spent months secluded in the White House living quarters wiring letters to her dead son. Life did go on, however, as the social notes on these pages show. Pierce's public service life was heavily influenced by his wife. A strong person who had moments of melan-choly, his wife's health was the priority in his life. She was described as delicate and a woman who didn't like public life. Her health, for example, forced Franklin to turn down an appointment to serve as attorney general in President James Polk's cabinet. Earlier, her health also caused him to resign his Senate seat and return to New Hampshire.

Pierce had little to show for his White House tenure and, consequently, Democrats turned to James Buchanan in 1857. The 14th president died 12 years later Oct. 8, 1869, at 65.

-- *From the Presidential Documents Collection of Ben Benson*

*The President
and Mrs Pierce,
request the favor of
Hon. John Letcher's
company at dinner
on thursday the 18th instant
at 6 O'Clock.*

A reply is requested.

This invitation issued by President & Mrs. Pierce to Governor Letcher of Lexington, Virginia. Governor Letcher was Governor of Virginia during the Civil War.

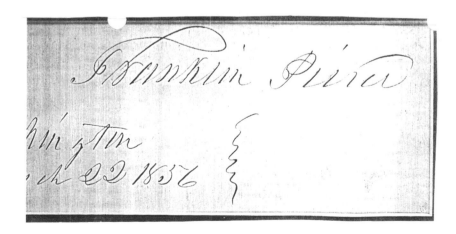

In another life, he could have been considered a pacifist. Man's duty was to submit to the will of God, he believed. And the turmoil of his presidency would have tested any responsible leader. During the tense, volatile years before the first cannon volleys at Fort Sumter, SC and the beginning of the Civil War, James Buchanan was considered a decent but aloof president who told the nation in his inaugural address, March 4, 1857:

"Having determined not to become a candidate for re-election, I shall have no motive to influence my conduct in administering the Government except the desire ably and faithfully to serve my country and to live in grateful memory of my countrymen."

A much younger Buchanan served as secretary of state to the politically astute James K. Polk, the 11th president. A shrewd expansionist, Polk used a war with Mexico to annex California and most of the Southwest.

The circular on this page shows the 32-year-old Buchanan's signature dated on his first day in the Polk Administration in 1845.

Considered a plodder, painstaking in detail but of average ability as a lawyer, Buchanan was scrupulous, however, in separating politics from finance. James Buchanan planned a life as a country squire practicing law shortly after he met and became engaged to a Pennsylvania socialite. He was devastated when her parents persuaded her to break off the relationship. She died a short time later and her passing changed his life. "I may sustain the shock of her death but I feel that happiness has fled from me, forever," he wrote her parents. He entered politics later to forget his grief, he told friends.

While always mindful of moral values, Buchanan, a bachelor, was, however, tempted to acquire bottles of "spirits." His companions said his country estate, called Wheatland, near Lancaster, PA, had a wine cellar well stocked with fine vintages. His taste for spirits was as strong as his interest as a connoisseur too. At formal parties Buchanan was observed downing a cognac which would be followed by two or even three bottles of wine. He would finish a party with several glasses of rye.

A church goer, Buchanan would use his Sunday drive to services to take a pit stop at a local distillery to buy ten-gallon casks of a whiskey called "Old J.B." Some guests thought his ample supply meant the distiller had named the brew for the president. But the brewer, whose names was Jacob Baer, merely smiled when asked. James Buchanan died June 1, 1868, at 77.

-- From the Presidential Documents Collection of Ben Benson

Circular.

Department of State
Washington, 10th March 1845

I have the honor to inform you that the President,
by and with the advice and consent of the Senate,
has appointed me Secretary of State of the United States,
and that I have this day entered upon the duties of that office.

I am, Sir,
Your obedient servant,

James Buchanan

To A. D. Mann.

U.S. Consul.

Bremen

Signed, first day in office as Secretary of State.

16th President 1861-1865 Two Terms

If there was a president who suffered abuse in office ... it was Abraham Lincoln. His wife Mary's mental instability led her to frequently tongue lash her husband and worse, his generals' vanities and bickering exasperated and pushed a non-military president to become an armchair strategist. His wartime decisions, frequently criticized by cabinet members and others, ultimately led to his assassination in the brief span of four years.

Volumes have been written about his life, his times and America's violent civil war. He wasn't a religious man as a number of his predecessors were yet he had a strong belief in predestination. And he demonstrated his respect for a higher power, too. In 1864, Lincoln wrote: "The purposes of the Almighty are perfect, and must prevail, though erring mortals may fail to accurately perceive. Surely He intends some great good to follow this mighty convulsion, which no mortal could make, and no mortal could stay." Lincoln truly thought he was in the hands of a higher power.

At the same time, he refused to lay down a gauntlet during a tense, incendiary period. As the nation crept inexorably closer to collapse over the slavery issue, he tried vainly to change attitudes.

"I have no purpose, directly or indirectly, to interfere with the institution of slavery in the states when it exists. I believe I have no lawful right to do so, and I have no inclination to do so," he told his inaugural audience, March 4, 1861.

But war came with Fort Sumter's guns a month later. By the time it ended at Appomattox forty-eight months later, more men had been killed than in any other American conflict since. He had tried every form of diplomacy to avoid such a holocaust. As his presidency started he told Americans that "we are not enemies, but friends. We must not be enemies. Though passion may have strained it must not break our bonds of affection."

Ben Benson gives you a glimpse of the emotion of the day -- an electoral ballot from Michigan appealing for "No Compromise With Treason" in 1864 -- when Lincoln and his running mate Andrew Johnson campaigned to defeat Union Army General George B. McClellan and his vice presidential candidate, G.H. Pendleton.

The re-elected president died on the same day he received word that Lee had surrendered; April 14, 1865. The weather in Washington was sunny and Lincoln, who had many bouts of depression, was in a good mood for a change. Some would have said it was a predestined day; Mary had a headache and suggested that they not go to Ford's Theatre that night. The president's bodyguard detachment was away on a mission but had expressly warned Lincoln not to go and Secretary of War Henry Stanton had also advised the president to avoid crowds. But Lincoln felt he had to go; his appearance had been announced in afternoon newspapers.

-- From the Presidential Documents Collection of Ben Benson

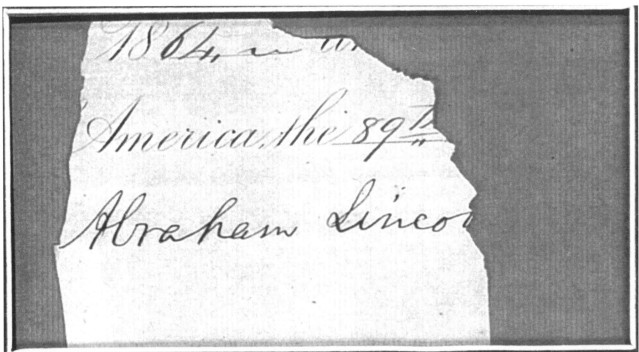

17th President 1865-1869

No question Andrew Johnson stood out in a crowd during the Civil War days in Washington. Sen. Johnson of Tennessee was the only southerner to remain loyal to the Union when 11 states, including his own, seceded.

It certainly made him politically appealing to President Lincoln who, in 1864, as parties prepared for a wartime election, thought the conflict between the North and South could last another three years. Lincoln and Johnson were kindred spirits. Both had come from poverty, both indicated that the South would rise once a plantation economy was removed and both were self-made men. It was Johnson's wife, Eliza, who taught him to read and write.

The one difference between the two leaders became pronounced when Lincoln died and Johnson became the 17th president. His stubborn refusal to show any compassion when circumstances warranted it was Johnson's Achilles heel. It had been Lincoln's strength.

The flaw surfaced months after Johnson took office. On a crucial Congressional campaign tour of the East and Midwest, he became rattled, defensive and belligerent with hecklers and agitators. Newspapers weren't sympathetic. Editors said he appeared "touched with insanity." To easterners it brought back memories of the Tennessean's frontier past when he ran for governor a decade earlier carrying a pistol and publicly declaring he'd use it.

Washingtonians still remembered that Johnson had appeared at the vice presidential inaugural drunk. His speech, observers said, was slurred and disjointed. The politically naive Johnson was suffering from an illness and a fever and had taken a good belt of whiskey to get through the ceremony. The liquor nearly floored him.

Impeachment dominated Johnson's last months. Though he submitted a Civil War Reconstruction plan similar to the one Lincoln had worked on before his death, Congress wanted little to do with the man or his program.

In a two month trial in the US Senate, the president was accused of everything from wrecking America to taking part in Lincoln's assassination plot. With 1,500 looking on in the packed gallery, a final ballot ended the impeachment. A young senator, Edmund Ross, from the country's newest state, Kansas, cast the deciding vote allowing Johnson to finish his term. Andrew Johnson died July 31, 1875, at 67.

-- From the Presidential Documents Collection of Ben Benson

BY THE PRESIDENT OF THE UNITED STATES.

A PROCLAMATION.

Whereas it has been the desire of the General Government of the United States to restore unrestricted commercial intercourse between and in the several States, as soon as the same could be safely done in view of resistance to the authority of the United States by combinations of armed insurgents;

And whereas that desire has been shown in my proclamations of the twenty-ninth of April, one thousand eight hundred and sixty-five, the thirteenth of June, one thousand eight hundred and sixty-five, and the twenty-third of June, one thousand eight hundred and sixty-five;

And whereas it now seems expedient and proper to remove restrictions upon internal, domestic, and coastwise trade and commercial intercourse between and within the States and Territories west of the Mississippi river:

Now, therefore, be it known that I, ANDREW JOHNSON, President of the United States, do hereby declare that all restrictions upon internal, domestic, and coastwise intercourse and trade, and upon the purchase and removal of products of States and parts of States and Territories heretofore declared in insurrection, lying west of the Mississippi river, (excepting only those relating to property heretofore purchased by the agents or captured by or surrendered to the forces of the United States, and to the transportation thereto or therein, on private account, of arms, ammunition, all articles from which ammunition is made—gray uniforms and gray cloth) are annulled; and I do hereby direct that they be forthwith removed; and also that the commerce of such States and parts of States shall be conducted under the supervision of the regularly appointed officers of the customs, [who] shall receive any captured and abandoned property that may be turned over to them, under the law, by the military or naval forces of the United States, and dispose of the same in accordance with instructions on the subject, issued by the Secretary of the Treasury.

In testimony whereof, I have hereunto set my hand, and caused the seal of the United States to be affixed.

[SEAL.]   Done at the City of Washington, this twenty-fourth day of June, in the year of our Lord one thousand eight hundred and sixty-five, and of the Independence of the United States of America the eighty-ninth.

ANDREW JOHNSON.

By the President:

W. HUNTER,
Acting Secretary of State.

PUBLIC DOCUMENT.
FREE.

U. S. S.

18th President 1869-1877, *two terms*

Biographer W.E. Woodward best summed up President Ulysses S. Grant's life: "He may have been a fool; he was also a genius. A pacifist at heart, he demanded 'unconditional surrender' of the confederacy. Though he could send thousands of men to their deaths, he could not bear to see an animal in pain. He drank heavily, but never swore. He was elected president -- but knew nothing of politics."

The two term presidency of another ex-general brought America to another crossroad that produced enormous excesses, corruption and, some historians wrote later, the worst scandals of the 18th century.

It was as novelist Charles Dickens, who had visited John Tyler in the White House in 1842, said in his famous book "A Tale of Two Cities," the best of times yet the worst of times. Fat cats became bloated and the public faced a wholesale theft of government services and tax dollars. Shy, sensitive and soft-spoken Grant was a study in contrasts. Smoking some 20 cigars a day, he won Lincoln's war by sheer numbers of soldiers killed. The former general lost 55,000 men in 30 days of battles.

Unfortunately, his wartime success was never matched in public life. He failed in farming, in real estate, in business and in the White House.

Vice President Schuyler Colfax's quote from the Ben Benson Collection on this page was significant. Colfax lifted a comment from Abraham Lincoln's Cooper Institute speech in 1860. It shows, in a way, the false illusion that troubled the Grant years. "Let us, have faith that right makes might and, in that faith let us, to the end, dare to do our duty." Some would have added that the public of that day was misled by whose right made "might."

Grant's work habits as president would have perplexed every president including Ronald Reagan who was known to take afternoon naps. He spent about four hours a day at his desk and didn't leave the family quarters to go to the office until mid-morning. Promptly at 3 p.m. daily he went to the White House horse stables where he spent time grooming his horses.

While the president kept his day free from long hours, his administration faced sordid scandals such as the Credit Mobilier which included Vice President Colfax, the resignation under pressure of his treasury secretary over a tax scheme, the Whiskey Ring conspiracy and the impeachment of his Secretary of War William W. Belknap over Indian Ring bribes.

The 18th president who said he believed in God in his own way, died July 23, 1885, at 63 a week after he finished the last chapter of his memoirs. He hoped his book would reduce the red ink of his estate which was marred by bankruptcy. He never saw a published copy of his book.

-- From the Presidential Documents Collection of Ben Benson

"Let us, have faith that Right makes Right; and, in that faith, let us, to the end, dare to do our Duty."

Lincoln; Cooper Institute speech, Feb. 1860.

Resp.y Yours,

Schuyler Colfax

Olathe, Kansas, May 4, 1878.

Quotation as hand-written by Schuyler Colfax, Vice-President under President Grant.

Quote is from A. Lincolns Cooper Institute Speech in New York City, February, 1860 during his first campaign for the presidency.

"Let us, have faith that right makes might and, in that faith let us, to the end, dare to do our duty."

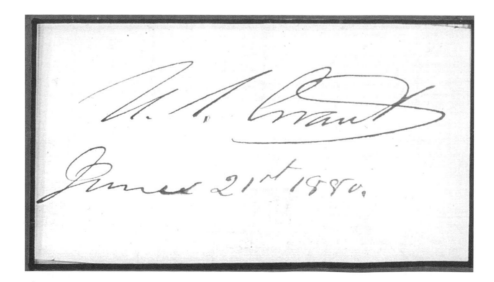

He wasn't the smartest or the most productive president but Rutherford B. Hayes could be considered one of the most technologically curious of 19th century chief executives.

Months after taking office, he heard late one night that inventor and fellow Ohioan, Thomas Edison, was in town. Ignoring the hour --- past 11 p.m. -- and that his wife Lucy had gone to bed, the president urged Edison to come over and bring his newest invention, the phonograph, with him. Edison entertained the president with his new talking machine playing the famous nursery rhyme, "Mary had a little lamb" until 3 in the morning.

It was Hayes who introduced the first telephone to the White House a year or so later. While it worked quite well, few others owned such a device so he really had no one to call in his third year, he installed the first typewriter and, unlike the correspondence shown on this page, presidential memoranda from that point appeared as printed lines instead of a calligrapher's cursive handwriting.

While considered an honest, Christian man, Hayes was a disappointment to many for failing to lead in making difficult but necessary legislative changes. Earlier in life, he summed up who he was. "I will never do anything inconsistent with the character of a true friend and good citizen," he wrote while attending Harvard Law School.

Mindful that his election was narrowly decided by one vote from a commission that declared him president months after the popular vote, Hayes is probably best remembered for trying to bring reform to civil service in federal government. But he couldn't get a balky Congress to agree.

The wealthiest president to occupy the office in the 19th century, Hayes and his wife, Lucy, were considered a model couple. He had served in the Civil War with the Ohio volunteers and had been wounded. Lucy, biographers noted, was very persuasive in the couple's decision making. She had a billiards table that US Grant had installed during his presidency removed and brought pressure to forbid alcohol in the White House ... even though her husband did drink.

Rutherford B. Hayes died in 1893 at age 71.

-- From the Presidential Documents Collection of Ben Benson

The President and Mrs. Hayes
request the pleasure of
The Secretary of the Treasury
and Mrs. Sherman's company
at dinner on Monday February
9th at seven o'clock.

To meet Mr. and Mrs. Tilton

Executive Mansion,
Feby. 2d 1880

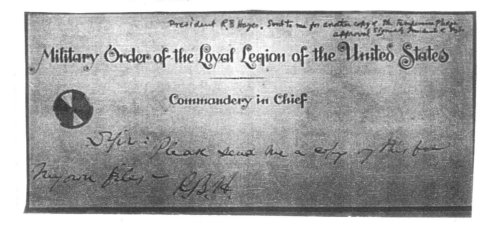

R B Hayes

Signature as President.

20th President, 1881

Some presidents entertained themselves during their lives playing cards, some played the piano, even the sax and some collected stamps. Not James A. Garfield; he amused himself translating Goethe poems from German to English.

Garfield, colleagues said, was a true intellectual of the boot strap variety. Among the last of the presidents from the Midwest born in a cabin, he drove canal boat teams to earn the tuition to attend Williams College. He returned to his native northern Ohio after graduating from Williams to teach the classics at Western Eclectic Institute - Hiram College today -- and impressed colleagues there, too.

Within a year, he was named one of the youngest college presidents in the country at 26.

As the Civil War spread across America, he again proved his leadership, this time on the battlefield. At 31, he became a brigadier general. In 1862, he won election to Congress from Ohio and won re-election nine times.

In Washington, his scholarly days behind him, he became a wily political pol who was a willing accomplice of the notorious Grant Administration. He was implicated in the scandals of 1870s but never smeared.

Later, he sat on the 1876 Presidential Election Commission that declared Rutherford B. Hayes the winner by a single vote.

His presidential candidacy was a surprise, even to him. He won the nomination on the 36th ballot. In a lackluster campaign that followed, Garfield beat General Winfield Scott Hancock by 10,000 votes. But his time in the White House was scuttled from the very beginning. He had to mend party unity with powerful New York Senator Roscoe Conkling of Utica who demanded control over the sprawling patronage system in New York City. Garfield, however, refused.

It was during these tense days that Garfield must have seen the hate boiling as the party feuded over its massive and lucrative patronage. Charles J. Guiteau did. A failed evangelist, he dreamed of a political future and, in his deranged mind, the president owed him. He appeared at the White House daily, convinced that the President must give him a federal appointment even at a time when Garfield was determined to have a merit system installed.

Ironically, Guiteau stalked Garfield during a day when the country still had horrible memories of the Ford Theater shooting of Abraham Lincoln who had a security detail no less! But Garfield didn't even have a bodyguard when Guiteau shot him twice in the back several days before the Fourth of July, 1881. The president lingered for more than two months before he died Sept. 19, at 50.

-- From the Presidential Documents Collection of Ben Benson

J. A. Garfield. Me

B. A. Hinsdale Esq.
Care Richard Hawley Eq
Detroit
Mich.

Mrs. Garfield's thanks
to Mr. Ellis B. Robt
for the photograph of
General Garfield's
brother, Mr Thomas Garfield,
And accept her kind
regard.
So Pasadena California
Feb. 27th 1910.

21st President, 1881-1885

Chester Arthur really looked and acted like a president ... which may have made him more vulnerable to his weaknesses than was realized. He was a Hollywood figure, impeccable dresser who loved the best wines and food and the good life and never wanted it to go away.

Appointed by US Grant to the powerful post of customs collector of the Port of New York City with its thousands of patronage jobs, Arthur was an enthusiastic supporter of the political payback system and he became one of those clever and successful politicians popular in the Roscoe Conkling wing of the Republican Party. All those images worked against the likeable, high rolling vice president when Garfield was assassinated. The assassin let it be known that he had killed President Garfield to advance Arthur and those who supported patronage.

The event and the aftermath had a powerful impact on Arthur when he became president. In the early months, he surprised friend and foe alike with his attention to honest decision-making and efficiency. Biographer Thomas C. Reeves said it best: "Though few would have guessed it of this urbane politician, Arthur was deeply emotional, and romantic person, capable of great loyalties and easily brought to tears"

Yet he didn't turn his back on his tastes. He worked stubbornly to upgrade the appearance of the White House which he compared to a third rate Manhattan hotel. During his four years he waged war with preservationists over his plans to demolish the White House and start over. He finally settled on an extensive remodeling of the house. Early in his presidential years, an Associated Press report circulated that the president had Bright's Disease, a fatal kidney illness. Arthur denied it but the family leaked information affirming the report just before his term was completed.

Said Publisher A.K. McClure at his death: "No man ever entered the Presidency so profoundly and widely distrusted, and no one ever retired ... more generally respected."

Chester Arthur died Nov. 18, 1886, at 57.

-- From the Presidential Documents Collection of Ben Benson

_____, and of the Independence of the United States

Chester A Arthur

Fredk T. Frelinghuysen
Secretary of State.

22nd & 24th President, 1885-1889, 1893-1897 *two terms*

The first 21 presidents could have been models for weight watcher ads when compared to the country's 22nd president, portly Grover Cleveland who catapulted to national attention and the presidency in a quick 36 months.

But it wasn't his 260 pound frame that won over special interest groups. It was the New York governor's hard-working, single-minded honesty that caught journalists' and the public's attention. The country was weary of arrogant Republicans, scandal and greed. A bachelor, Cleveland took on his Democratic Party's Tammany Hall political machine and demonstrated that the corruption that had continued since the 1830s could be contained. He was a reformer whose efforts attracted Republicans, called "Mugwamps," as well as party regulars to his cause.

It certainly wasn't his charm, political observers said. An introverted personality, he could be stubborn to exasperation and he wouldn't hesitate to battle anyone he felt was wasteful or dishonest regardless of their position or party. Yet, his blunt honesty was so refreshing at the time. When Republicans found the sensational political story about Cleveland allegedly fathering an illegitimate child ("Ma, ma where's my pa?"), Democrats were anxious over the right response. "Tell the truth," Cleveland insisted and his forthright reaction won the day. A respected minister, the Rev. Kinsley Twining, investigated the charge and added more strength to Cleveland's honesty. "After the preliminary offense (Cleveland's) conduct was singularly honorable, showing no attempt to evade responsibility, and doing all that he could to meet the duties involved, of which marriage was certainly no one." Rev. Twining's conclusion virtually gave the president a good conduct pass.

The president struck that public chord that included common sense, frugality and antielitism that people of the day sought. He said it best in his Inaugural Address: "We should never be ashamed of the simplicity and prudential economies which are best suited to the operation of a republican form of government and most compatible with the mission of the American people."

He would have brought smiles to a 21st century American, too, when he offered a friend his view of French food. "I must go to dinner but I wish it was to eat a pickled herring, a Swiss cheese and a chop at Louis' instead of the French stuff I shall find."

His first term brought a change in his own life and in the country's challenge to meet problems head on. A year after entering the White House, he married Francis Folsom, a Wells College graduate about 27 years his junior, the first president to marry in office. The Clevelands spent most of their Washington years at a year-round retreat called "Red Top" on the outskirts of the city.

Politically, Cleveland gave capital watchers more to chew on than had been seen in years. He vetoed

304 bills in his first term, more than all of his predecessors' totals combined. His thoroughness was maddening ... but respected. Civil War pension bills had been sailing through Congress as the nation tried to show its appreciation for those who fought and to help veterans meet their needs. Previous presidents had signed them frequently without reading the contents.

Not Cleveland. He not only read each bill, he discovered patently false claims and refused to sign them. Furthermore, he made his appointees to government take merit tests ... not party affiliation. Nor would he hesitate to veto an appropriation request he felt wasn't honestly prepared. He angered railroad interests by demanding an investigation of land they held via government grants in the west. He forced them to relinquish 81 million acres. Later, he signed the first law establishing the Interstate Commerce Act, an attempt to regulate the railroads.

Defeated by the electoral not the popular vote in 1888, he said he left a happy man pleased by first term accomplishments. Cleveland fought back and won the rematch with President Benjamin Harrison in 1892. However, it was a more turbulent nation in the midst of economic disarray and impatient with tight fiscal programs that he faced after his inaugural address, March, 1893.

His own life had changed, too. While honest with his views he was obsessively private about his health. He secretly underwent surgery for the removal of a cancerous upper jaw in the early days of his second term.

He could do little about the Panic of '93 although he continued to battle to maintain services and public order. He sent federal troops to battle the Pullman Strike of 1894. Consistent with his view of honesty first, he announced his support of rival party candidate William McKinley near the final days of his presidency and his party, which had ignored him, virtually deserted him.

Grover Cleveland died June 24, 1908 at 71.

-- From the Presidential Documents Collection of Ben Benson

Rare:
Earliest known example of a White House Vignette signed and dated by a First Lady.
Mrs. Cleveland when signing this card was the youngest First Lady in the history of the White House. She was 22 years old, at this signing, 7 months after her marriage to President Cleveland in the White House.

His last name helped him and his campaign strategy gave him an added boost, said those who knew him. His personality wasn't especially attractive up close and personal, some said. The strategy to elect Benjamin Harrison, grandson of the 9th president, William Henry Harrison? Conduct a "front porch" campaign from his Indiana home. He was most adept at short speeches ... not meeting people.

Although Grover Cleveland got a 100,000 popular vote plurality, Harrison walked away with the electoral votes and won the presidency. Fifty-five-year-old Benjamin Harrison was thought to have capitalized on a statement by the British ambassador to Washington who remarked that Grover Cleveland would probably be more friendly to Britain than Harrison. At a time when tariffs were important issues, the comment influenced the American election, some historians believe.

An Ohioan who served as a colonel in the Indiania Volunteers during the Civil War, Harrison moved to Indianapolis and made a name for himself as an attorney. Elected to the Senate, he championed popular causes; homesteaders, Indians and Civil War veterans.

In the White House in March, 1889, he told his fellow citizens he didn't "mistrust the future." He conducted a strong campaign for foreign policy and was influential in the 1st Pan American Congress meeting to be held in the Capital. He submitted a treaty to annex Hawaii only to have his successor, Grover Cleveland, withdraw it.

He pushed Congress for appropriations to pursue internal improvements, naval expansion and even subsidies for steamship lines. Congressional bodies approved and critics called the legislature "the billion dollar Congress."

Harrison signed the Sherman Anti-Trust Act to protect trade and commerce in 1890 after warning American business leaders in his inaugural address that "if our great corporations would more scrupulously observe their legal limitations and duties, they would have less cause to complain of the unlawful limitations of their rights or of violent interference with their operations. The community that by concert, open or secret, among its citizens denies to a portion of its members their plain rights under the law has severed the only safe bond of social order and prosperity. The evil works from a bad center both ways." While lawyers later found ways to circumvent the anti-trust act ... Harrison attempted to put corporate leaders on notice.

The tariff issue, however, would be the president's Achilles heel. He tried to make the tariff more acceptable by adding reciprocity measures. But the US treasury surplus began eroding and the Democrats won the midterm elections.

His first wife, Caroline, took the task of becoming first lady with excitement. She believed the

White House needed refurbishing and launched her own plan to add two more wings to the building. The Senate, however, turned her down. Two weeks before the election of 1892, she died.

Harrison died March 13, 1901, at 68.

-- From the Presidential Documents Collection of Ben Benson

EXECUTIVE MANSION,
WASHINGTON.

Caroline Scott Harrison

Mr. Benjamin Harrison

and

Mrs. Mary Scott Dimmick

announce their marriage

on Monday, April the sixth,

eighteen hundred and ninety-six, at

Saint Thomas's Church,

New York.

Benj Harrison

In a Union army that was rife with corruption, sex and other vices, William McKinley must have been some kind of saint to many. Biographers report he enlisted as a private, was never heard swearing nor seen drinking or smoking during his four year tour of duty. He was a true Christian gentleman in hard-drinking US Grant's Army of the Potomac.

His virtues, of course, paid a lifetime of dividends. He mustered out of the service a major in Rutherford Hayes Ohio 23rd Volunteers.

William McKinley worked hard to build such an image and in post-war Ohio politics he easily outdistanced rivals. A Niles, OH native, he returned to nearby Canton, studied law, opened a practice and married the daughter of a prominent banking family, Ida Saxton.

His exemplary behavior won him a seat in Congress at 34 after serving as Stark County, OH District Attorney. He remained an Ohio congressman for 12 years. He later served two terms as governor of the Buckeye state, too. His work as a member of the powerful House Ways and Means Committee gave him an opportunity to explore tariff legislation although he admitted his real interest was for conversational purposes not to be an expert.

But his congeniality and experience made him an excellent choice for the Republican ticket to win back the White House in 1896. He even received a late endorsement from onetime Democratic standard bearer, Grover Cleveland. Thanks to wealthy Clevelander Marc Hanna, eastern interests and a country still cautious but undecided about the money question, the Republicans defeated polished orator William Jennings Bryan by nearly 600,000 votes.

McKinley moved into 1600 Pennsylvania Avenue with Americans cautiously confident. The President called the Congress into Special Session and one of the highest tariff acts in history was passed.

People generally responded to his dignified, "full dinner pail" campaign because he demonstrated to them that he was a warm hearted, sentimentalist down deep, not an economic guru (which he was not). Yet he made clear in his inaugural what the public could understand about the economy: "If revenues are to remain as now, the only relief that can come must be from decreased expenditures ... the Government should not be permitted to run behind." In foreign affairs, McKinley followed Cleveland's 1895 policy of non-interference with Spain over Cuba but public pressure mounted and the unexplained sinking of the Maine and loss of 250 sailors in February, 1898, brought the inevitable war. The president, historians have maintained over the years, pandered the war issue although advisers knew he was truly against such a conflict.

In other diplomatic regions, he brought about the annexation of Hawaii in 1897 and he worked to bring an open door policy to China.

McKinley's life in later years was complicated by his wife's painful pregnancies which ended in the death of his two sons. She never recovered from the experience and developed an unexplained epilepsy. One of the reasons McKinley didn't campaign in 1896 against the aggressive and eloquent Bryan was he refused to leave his wife's side during her illness. White House state and social dinners could be very awkward, observers said, because Mrs. McKinley could have a seizure at any moment. The president and the wait staff worked out a plan so that he would always sit next to her with a large napkin close by. He would quickly place the napkin over her face and head to make sure guests didn't see her transfixed eyes and the foam gurgling from her mouth.

An assassin's bullet cut down the 25th president as his term ended. A secret service detail combined with a Buffalo police squad couldn't prevent Leon Czolgosz, an anarchist, from shooting McKinley, Sept. 6, 1901. Agents had changed the rules of protection because it was such a sweltering day and Czolgosz covered his gun hand with a handkerchief to fire off two shots.

The president died eight days after the shooting, Sept. 14,1901. He was 58.

-- From the Presidential Documents Collection of Ben Benson

Letter as President/Elect.

WILLIAM McKINLEY
CANTON OHIO

Nov. 12th, 1896,

Hon. Henry C. Taylor,

Columbus, O.,

My Dear Mr. Taylor:-

For your congratulations and good wishes to myself and Mrs. McKinley, we return our sincere thanks.

Very truly yours,

W. McKinley

26th President 1901-1909 Two Terms

After generations of elder statesmen occupied the presidency, the sudden death of President William McKinley catapulted a brash, 42-year-old Theodore Roosevelt to the White House in one traumatic September week in 1901.

Roosevelt was the youngest president in US history (John F. Kennedy was the youngest elected to the office at 43). The trauma for Americans came not only in the death of the chief executive, it came in the collision of styles, age, upbringing and temperament of the two personalities.

McKinley adviser Marc Hanna viewed young Roosevelt with distrust. He believed the vice president would be a disaster as president.

Roosevelt, obviously, saw the tragedy as an opportunity to innovate; he wanted to lead Congress and the American people on a righteous mission toward progressive reform and a much stronger foreign policy.

The new president, who liked to be referred to as TR not Teddie, saw himself as the "steward of the people" with the authority to act for the public good wherever and whenever unless prohibited by law or the constitution. "I did not usurp power ... but I did greatly broaden the use of executive power" he later wrote.

From the time the transferal of power took place on the afternoon of McKinley's death Sept. 14 in Buffalo change was obvious. McKinley was the last of the Civil War veterans from American's rural Midwest and log cabin past, TR was a city guy born into wealth from New York City whose life had been much different. A sickly, asthmatic childhood had been overcome with a strenuous life of boxing, hiking, horseback riding, hunting and two years running cattle ranches in the Badlands of the Dakotas.

But he proved his intellectual prowess, too. A magna cum laude Harvard graduate, he later lost interest in law studies at Columbia and plunged into New York State politics instead.

While McKinley had opposed war with Spain until it became inevitable, TR welcomed conflict and he distinguished himself as a lieutenant colonel with the First Cavalry Regiment, better remembered as the Rough Riders. Though the regiment saw limited action, Roosevelt's gallantry at the Battle of San Juan Heights brought a nomination for the Congressional Medal of Honor. It was denied but a century later, he was posthumously awarded the Medal of Honor for his valor.

Roosevelt pledged to honor McKinley's pro-business policies but he had already abandoned them within months. In a year, his administration filed the first 45 anti-trust suits starting with a major litigation against the Northern Securities rail trust of powerful J.P. Morgan.

Within days he unveiled his dedication to preservation and conservation when he signed the Newlands Reclamation Act that launched 21 federal irrigation projects in western United States. During his eight years in office, more then 125 million acres of woodlands were protected from development.

His plans and programs, radically different than his running mate years earlier, captured America, however. He established two federal departments, Commerce and Labor, to bring government into the country's economic growth. His dynamic style and flair dominated Democrat Alton Parker in the election of 1904.

After issuing the "Roosevelt Corollary" to the Monroe Doctrine, TR finished his calculated effort to acquire land and water passage between Americas by negotiating with Columbia to buy land in its northern most province and construct the Panama Canal. His methods and audacity angered many inside and out of his administration. When Roosevelt gave his cabinet members his plan to defend the acquisition, Secretary of War Elihu Root retorted: "You have shown that you were accused of seduction, and you have conclusively proved that you were guilty of rape."

Married twice, TR's first wife died from complications of childbirth ... the same day he lost his mother to typhoid fever. His second wife Edith, a childhood sweetheart, was more serious, temperamental and intellectual, friends said.

A prodigious researcher and writer, TR published his first book, "Hunting Trips of a Ranchman,' in1885. Over the next 34 years he would write and publish 21 historical and outdoors books.

He left office in March, 1909, took on a number of domestic and world projects but still longed for the power of the White House. When the Republicans renominated William Howard Taft for re-election although Roosevelt had won all but one primary, TR and other reformers launched the "Bullmoose" Party in August, 1912. In the heat of the three-way race between Taft, Woodrow Wilson and Roosevelt, TR is shot outside a Milwaukee hotel. The unflappable Bullmoose Party candidate refuses medical attention and gives a 90-minute speech before he goes to the hospital to have the bullet removed.

Theodore Roosevelt died in his sleep January 6, 1919, at 61 after losing his youngest son in World War I months earlier and refusing a nomination for governor of New York.

-- From the Presidential Documents Collection of Ben Benson

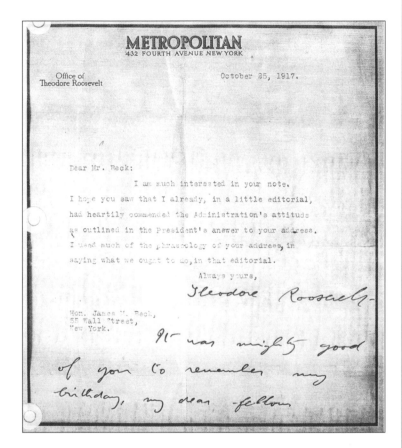

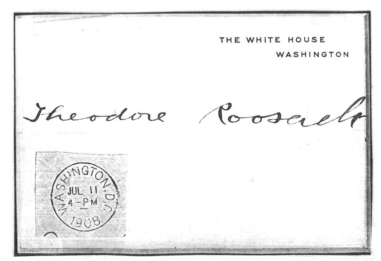

If there was a president who earned the position through loyalty and efficiency, not politics, it was affable William Howard Taft.

Considered a poor politician who hated campaigning, Taft's redeeming values were his effectiveness as an administrator and his conscientious devotion to friends and duty. A McKinley protégé, Taft fit easily with the flamboyant, demanding and impulsive Roosevelt. A roly poly bureaucrat, he rose through Republican ranks from his native Ohio to Washington handling administrative appointments.

McKinley dispatched him to the Philippines as chief administrator in 1900 where he won respect for involving Philipinos in charting the development of their country. At the same time, he improved the country's economy, built roads and opened new schools. Roosevelt named him secretary of war and he served as the president's frequent emissary during their years together.

TR could have run and probably won a third term given his popularity and youth (50) but instead he took time off to spend a year on an African safari and help Taft handily win a landslide victory over William Jennings Bryan. Bryan was a third time loser for the Democrats.

Taft's victory, however, left him dancing precariously on the edge of a political sword. TR returned from Africa convinced that his hand-picked successor wasn't progressive enough. At the same time, the Republican Stand-Patters, the eastern wing of the party, urged the president to stand firm against those who wanted constant change. Roosevelt's invective became so harsh that the two men never renewed their friendship again.

The 27th president's days in the White House called for staff ingenuity, too. There were always changes when new presidents and their families took over the living quarters and the management of the mansion at 1600 Pennsylvania Avenue. Furniture would be re-arranged, new room décor was always inevitable, paintings would be moved ... but this was the first time recorded that the staff had to find a new bathtub. To accommodate the 300 to 350 pound president, a new tub, 7 feet by nearly 4 feet that weighed a ton had to be installed ... at taxpayer's expense.

While Roosevelt made it clear he would stretch his executive powers if he had to, Taft wouldn't and his refusal infuriated liberal Republicans. As hard as he tired to please all sides, his conscientious efforts backfired. When he defended higher tariffs, the progressives bolted. Further, his support of his secretaries of the interior Richard Ballinger and Franklin Lane from an attack by TR that they weren't enthusiastically supporting his conservation programs also brought anger from the former president. In reality, Taft's Administration pursued 80 anti-trust suits --- nearly double the number of Roosevelt's two terms --- it initiated income tax and directed the Interstate Commerce Commission to set rail rates as well as set up a postal savings system.

Roosevelt, however, was eager to get back to the White House and he split with the Republican Party to help create the Progressive Party in 1912. His efforts probably helped Democrat Woodrow Wilson become the 28th president.

Taft, meanwhile, introduced a presidential custom that has continued to this day. He was the first president to not only play golf but encourage the sport. The largest president, Taft believed that golf would help him lose weight. It didn't ... but he never stopped believing. According to the New York Times in June 1909, his efforts had helped the number of those playing the game increase.

Seventy-three-old William Howard Taft died March 8, 1930.

-- From the Presidential Documents Collection of Ben Benson

THE WHITE HOUSE
WASHINGTON

Mrs. Taft regrets that she cannot comply with Mr. Jones' request as all the cherry trees which were sent her had to be destroyed on account of being infected with dangerous diseases.
January 31st 1910.

First Lady Helen Taft

Rare: Hand written letter as First Lady in regards to the famous Japanese Cherry Trees.

Mrs. Taft was responsible for the planting of the Cherry Trees. Today, the spring Cherry Blossoms are one of the most popular tourist attractions.

This letter refers to first shipment which had to be destroyed due to disease.

28th President 1913-1921 Two Terms

He was a scholar and a teacher. He had more degrees than any of his predecessors. He taught government, headed one of America's most respected universities and was called "Schoolmaster of Politics."

Woodrow Wilson, recent governor of New Jersey and past president of Princeton, demonstrated to party polls and the public he wasn't simply an academic ... he was his own man. He distanced himself from conservatives in New Jersey, for example, and endorse a progressive platform.

When nominated by Democrats to run for the presidency in 1912 he stressed individualism and states' rights in a platform he shaped called "New Freedom." He won the three-way race with 42 percent of the popular vote but an overwhelming number of electorate ballots.

Yet, he was, without question, a man of paradoxes. A stern, cold person in public, he loved family life, parlor games and a kind of natural silliness that the average person rarely saw. At the same time, he could be unbending and righteous in conducting business of state.

His eight year term of office was momentous in the country's history. Entangled with it there was tragedy, too. His first wife, Ellen, died of Bright's disease. She was considered his closest adviser. His need for companionship was so strong that he abandoned the respectable mourning period and by the end of the second year was preparing to marry his second wife, Edith.

Both wives played important roles in the Wilson presidency. They were known to have read documents that he took home at nights and offered advice when it was sought. Edith wasn't considered the intellectual but her role was even more critical when the 62-year-old president, near exhaustion from a trip to Europe for the Paris Peace Conference, returned home to make a speech making tour of the country to support the Treaty of Versailles. He suffered a stroke in October , 1919. Some contend and have written that Edith became de facto president during Wilson's final days in office. "I studied every paper ... and tried to digest and present in tabloid form the things that, despite my vigilance, had to go to the president," Edith wrote. A delegate of the Senate Foreign Relations Committee including friend and enemy appeared at the White House more than a month after he had been confined to bed. Demonstrating his strength of character, the president let them know he hadn't lost his sense of presence or sardonic humor. When told that the Senate members were praying for him ... Wilson shot back "which way, Senator?"

His knowledge of politics helped him work with Congress. During his first term he brought about the Underwood Act which introduced a lower tariff and added a graduated income tax. He helped Congress accept a Federal Reserve Act to provide a growing money supply desperately needed. In 1914, he added to anti-trust legislation by creating the Federal Trade Commission. His administration also produced a new law prohibiting child labor and another piece of legislation which limited railroad workers to an eight hour day. Some believe that this particular legislation and the slogan "he kept us out of war" (referring to the war in Europe) was what helped forge the coalition of labor, farmers, reformers and intellectuals that gave him victory in 1916.

Months later, German attacks on allied shipping and its refusal to mediation caused Wilson to ask Congress for a declaration of war "to make the world safe for democracy." After an armistice in November 1918, Wilson issued his celebrated 14 point plan for a just peace. His peace plan was nearly scuttled by those abroad and the Senate at home. Failing health left him to end his two terms frustrated by his own country's unwillingness to enter into a European alliance for peace called the "League of Nations."

He died in Washington, DC Feb. 1924 at 68.

-- From the Presidential Documents Collection of Ben Benson

WOODROW WILSON
W. STATE ST., TRENTON, N. J.

November 13, 1912.

My dear little Friend:

I cannot tell you what gratification it gives me that you should think of me. Your letter has given me a great deal of genuine pleasure, and I hope that as the years go on you will continue to feel that I am the sort of man you would like to support and keep as your friend.

Cordially and faithfully yours,

Woodrow Wilson

Miss Mildred White,
    Chambersburg, Pa.

Letter written as President/Elect.

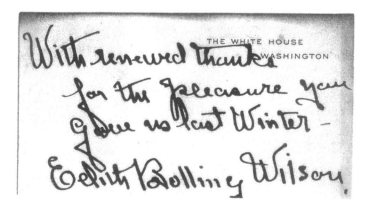

Warren G. Harding's musical talent gives us a glimpse at his political acumen and outlook, too. He once organized a Citizen's Band in his hometown of Marion, OH which was available, he insisted, to Democratic as well as Republican rallies. "I played every instrument but the slide trombone and the E-flat trumpet," he told a gathering explaining how far he'd go to help his friends. A distinguished looking man, his private secretary said it was estimated that the president shook hands with more than 250,000 people during his political career.

Harding could engage people easily yet he wasn't charismatic. As editor of the Marion (OH) Star, he was probably the most popular president among correspondents and news people in the country's history. He knew most reporters by their first names which may also have been a reason a number of his problems didn't get attention from the media. He considered loyalty a virtue but later fell sharply from public respect because of the trust he placed in untrustworthy aides and advisors.

His public charm and ease, which some believed masked his vanity, diluted a multitude of unpopular vices at the time. While Prohibition was the law of the land, Harding drank ... sometimes to excess. The president, who was rarely photographed or seen with a drink in his hand, appears to have paid lip service to the law which he voted for. His regular poker parties at the White House were also distasteful ... even in the eyes of some of his advisers. His Secretary of Commerce, Herbert Hoover, was so shocked he never returned to the White House games after one evening of playing.

But by far his reported trysts with young Nan Britton , thirty years is junior, in the White House raised many more eyebrows even though nothing of such activities appeared in the press while he lived.

Hardings' life was a study in contrasts. A good speaker with a pleasant voice, his charming manners hid his inability to be independent of the machine bosses from Ohio to Washington. A trustee of the community's conservative Baptist Church, he married Mrs. Florence DeWolfe, a rich divorcee, who contributed the money to rebuild Harding's struggling newspaper.

To politicians of the time and historians years later who placed the Ohioan at the bottom of America's list of presidents, he totally misread the public mood and his party's attitude toward Woodrow Wilson's vision of collective security with the League of Nations. Thirty-one important Republicans signed a declaration to voters pledging that Harding would vote for the League. Instead, he interpreted his overwhelming victory of 60 percent of the popular vote as the reason United States would stay out of the League. As his term progressed, one of his campaign slogans --

- "Less government in business and more business in government" --- seemed very appropriate. A return to normalcy made everyone feel good, he felt.

Scattered rumors about insider mismanagement and corruption became louder in the months before the end of his tenure. In 1923, Harding took his conservative Secretary of Commerce Hoover with him on a western swing. He died Aug. 2, 1923, of a heart attack in California at 58.

Presidential historian and author of the Foreword of this book, Robert Ferrell, refutes a number of the allegations made about Harding and his place in presidential history. In his book, "The Strange Deaths of President Harding" (Missouri Press/1998) Ferrell claimed that Harding's high blood pressure and great stress were the true causes of death not the alleged poisoning by his wife that some speculated. Ferrell said there was also no proof of an illegitimate child in the president's relationship with Nan Britton as was suggested. Furthermore, the author pointed out, Harding did not know the particulars of the scandals building momentum around the White House even though several of his friends committed suicide to avoid prosecution months later.

-- From the Presidential Documents Collection of Ben Benson

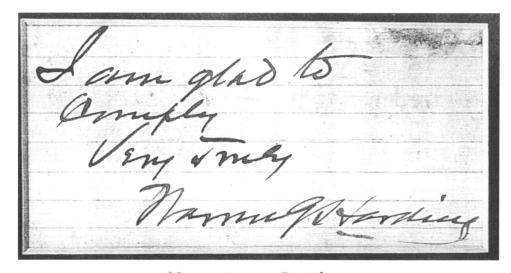

Note written as President.

How Calvin Coolidge and Warren Harding ended up on the same ticket in 1921 is still bewildering. They were as different as William Howard Taft and Theodore Roosevelt ... and then some.

Coolidge, one historian wrote, "was about as far from Harding's good fellowship as we could get." A White House guest after meeting Coolidge one night, said his smile "was like ice breaking up in a New England river."

However, after the Harding Administration's image plunged in one sordid scandal after another, Coolidge's thrift, stability and caution seemed a blessing to many Americans.

The 30th president took the oath of office in much the same way TR did after McKinley was assassinated. News of Harding's death on the west coast went to Washington first and then it was routed to tiny Bridgewater, VT, the closest telegraph office to Coolidge's father's home in Plymouth Notch where the vice president and his family were vacationing.

Coolidge was urged by Secretary of State Charles E. Hughes to take the oath of office right away and his father, a notary public, administered the pledge to his son by flickering kerosene lamp light at 2:47 a.m. He signed the forms in triplicate ... and went back to bed.

The United States entered the next six years as a period of status quo-ism with Coolidge at the helm. A democratic rival gave an admiring appraisal of the president's efforts. The president, said Al Smith, was "distinguished for character more than heroic achievement. His great task was to restore the dignity and prestige of the Presidency when it had reached the lowest ebb in our history ... in a time of extravagance and waste. . ."

Coolidge did what he did best; he was determined to hold on to old moral and economic tenets and, by 1924, "Coolidge's prosperity" was thought to be working. It was so good, in fact, he captured more than 54 percent of the popular vote in the November election.

In his first speech to Congress, December, 1923, he offered his recipe for America; isolation from foreign entanglements, tax cuts and limited aid to farmers ... In his inaugural months later, it was clearly more of the same.

Political analyst Walter Lippmann said it succinctly: "This inactivity suits the mood and certain of the needs of the country admirably ... it suits all those who have become convinced that government in this country has become dangerously complicated and top-heavy ..."

While Coolidge was obviously the president who spoke the fewest words, he could have been considered the most congenial resident of 1600 Pennsylvania Avenue. He showed great patience posing in Indian headdress, blankets, cowboy hats and boots and other unbecoming costumes for photographers.

Unlike his predecessors who, in leaving office expended volumes of verbiage, Coolidge was typically "Silent Cal" upon his departure. His final public utterance? "I do not choose to run for President in 1928." He died Jan. 5, 1933 at 61.

-- From the Presidential Documents Collection of Ben Benson

Mourning letters sent of President & Mrs. Coolidge. Both letters are dated August 11, 1923, 9 days after the death of President Harding. The Black-bordered stationary used for only 28 days of official mourning. Of the two mourning letters, Grace Coolidge is the rarest, no other example is known to exist.

Photo Postcard- On front, President Coolidge has inscribed & signed to: Dakota Clyde Jones. It was this time that President Coolidge issued his 1927 Terse Statement "I do not wish to run for the Presidency in 1928." Rapid City, South Dakota

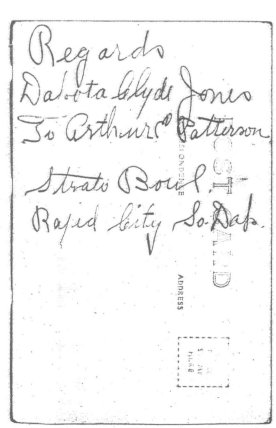

31st President 1929-1933

If there was one aspect of government Herbert Hoover understood it was organizing and managing relief services. He spent nearly 15 years at home and abroad trying to assist people in need. He even spent a month under hostile fire in the Boxer Rebellion in China trying to build barricades.

But his presidency, although it started with an assumption of prosperity, was one of the worst economic times in American history. Within months after he won and took office, the stock market crashed and the country started a progressive slide into an economic oblivion.

He made clear his position about government involvement in the economy just before he won the presidency the previous November. He had seen enough anarchy, corruption and abusive rule abroad, he said. "Even if governmental conduct of business could give us more efficiency instead of less efficiency, the fundamental objection to it would remain unaltered and unabated. It would increase rather than decrease abuse and corruption."

While Hoover didn't cause the collapse of the American marketplace, political writers like William Allen White and others saw the president as a "low voltage" personality trying to deal a very "high voltage" problem that affected all Americans.

Midway through his term, the United States had become a nation of so-called "Hooverville" shanty towns forthe homeless. While Coolidge had seen a 1.6 million growth in employment several years earlier, Hoover watched 7.7 million lose their jobs; a 9 percent drop.

Though the Republican Administration was sharply criticized for its lack of response and inertia in dealing with the difficulties of average Americans, Hoover did try to take action. He asked Congress for tax cuts, expanded public works spending and the creation of a Reconstruction Finance Corporation to aid business, help farmers, bring about banking reform and permit loans to the states to help the unemployed. Yet, he insisted, he wanted to help people find ways to meet the needs in their own communities.

Opponents in Congress seized on what was perceived as the president's indifference. The body tried to sabotage his ideas and paint them as cruel. A one-time humanitarian was portrayed as the person who created America's economic disaster.

His wife, Lou, was the ideal mate for Hoover. Tomboyish, unconventional, she took on the task of recording a history of the White House using her own monies to hire a photographer.

At the same time, she did create a minor stir for the president when she invited the wife of a Black congressman to a White House tea and was denounced by southern editors.

The Texas legislature, in fact, formally censured her.

Herbert Hoover died Oct. 20, 1964 at 90.

-- From the Presidential Documents Collection of Ben Benson

Hoover's scarce hand-written notes on application for "Who's Who."

32nd President 1933-1945 Four Terms

The first and only president to be elected four terms, Franklin Roosevelt took office during a national economic crisis and died in office just days before the German surrender that ended World War II in Europe.

To many, Roosevelt was the driving force behind America's recovery from its worst economic depression that put 13 million out of work and closed thousands of banks and businesses to fighting a war that struck a devastating blow to a US territory. When Herbert Hoover failed to rally people and Congress to action, Roosevelt, who uttered that famous phrase "the only thing we have to fear is fear itself" at his inaugural address, brought sweeping changes in his first 100 days.

By 1935, his drastic reforms --- relief to the unemployed, help for farmers and businesses, establishments of a Tennessee Valley Authority, Works Progress Administration, Social Security and other "New Deal" programs -- had brought acceptance as well as division in America.

The public idolized the gritty aristocrat and his courageous fight to live and work with polio that struck him at 39. He was putting food on their tables and providing income for families that had nowhere to turn. Businessmen, by contrast, were fearful of the unknown. FDR's policies brought deficits, made concessions to labor, brought higher taxes to the wealthy, put controls on banks and utilities, and mounted enormous relief expenditures.

It was no surprise to observers that FDR brought flashbacks of his fifth cousin, TR, whom he admired.

He was re-elected by a large margin in 1936 and he used the mandate to bring political pressure to enlarge the Supreme Court that had struck down some of his New Deal programs. He lost the battle with the courts, but the issue brought a new government ability to regulate the economy.

Roosevelt launched a "Good Neighbor" policy to complement the Monroe Doctrine and he arranged for mutual defense agreements against aggressors. But he walked a careful line to keep US out of the treacherous slide toward war in Europe. At the same time, he acted to strengthen US allies. The fall of France in 1940 brought increased aid to Britain. The Japanese attack on Pearl Harbor, Dec. 7, 1941, brought instant US reaction and a transformation of America from peacetime to wartime. Critics and some historians, however, believe Roosevelt was far more knowledgeable of Japanese intentions than the public realized. In his book "Day of Deceit: The Truth About FDR and Pearl Harbor," Robert B. Stinnett (Free Press/2000) questions official pronouncements given documents made available years later through the Freedom of Information Act. Other authors have suggested similar possibilities. The argument continues today.

While Roosevelt was a popular wartime leader who enjoyed overwhelming support from a bipartisan Congress and the public, his Japanese Relocation Order of Feb. 19, 1942, which evacuated some 112,000 West Coast Japanese was considered a flagrant act of human rights violation. Said E. S. Corwin, a political commentator of FDR's decision, it was the most drastic invasion of the rights of citizens of the US by their own government that has occurred in the history of our nation."

   Like other presidents earlier and later, FDR's marriage was rocky. It was kept together, many believe, by a strong wife, Eleanor, who swallowed his dalliances for the sake of their children and his political career. Her public service career as a spokesperson for civil rights, labor, tenant farmers, women and the poor continued long after she had left the White House.

   Franklin D. Roosevelt died April 12, 1945, at 63.

-- From the Presidential Documents Collection of Ben Benson

Signed first day of third Inaugural.

R BENSON
1971

Harry Truman must have felt some kinship with Vice President John Tyler who didn't know President Harrison had died in 1841 until two messengers knocked at his door and told him a day later. Similar to Tyler's first day on the job, nobody had kept Truman in the loop either.

For example, he didn't know about the $2 billion, three-year atomic weapon project in the New Mexico desert. And he had little knowledge of our growing difficulties with Russia. He told reporters: "I felt like the moon, the stars, and all the planets had fallen on me."

His life for 61 years had been a homespun variety of farming, small business, World War I service in the artillery and various local and state political positions as a Missouri democrat closely allied to Midwest political boss James Prendergast. As a US senator, he became involved in investigating waste and corruption linked to the war effort. He helped bring about some $15 billion in savings.

But Truman's most important role came in mid-1945 as the US struggled to avoid a major assault on the Japanese homeland that seemed inevitable and could lead to the loss of thousands of lives of soldiers and civilians. The US had informally offered the Japanese a chance to surrender .. and had been turned down. The president consulted his advisers and decided that the only alternative was to drop two atomic bombs on the cities considered still involved in the Japanese war effort; Hiroshima and Nagasaki. The Japanese surrendered unconditionally a short time later.

Days before he made the decision, a number of historians have suggested was one of the most difficult a president has ever made, Truman observed the signing of the Charter of the United Nations.

With the end of the war in the fall, 1945, the clamor to bring troops home and return to peaceful enterprises created a need for Truman policies, not a continuation of his popular predecessor.

He gave Congress an ambitious 21-point report on Social Security, a Fair Employment Practices Act, a full employment plan and remedies for public housing and slum clearance. It was Truman's "Fair Deal."

But nobody, including the Chicago Daily Tribune that carried an embarrassing early edition heading that Dewey had won the 1948 election, thought the blunt-speaking, ex-piano player could beat a smooth talking New Yorker like Dewey, a well-respected crime busting prosecutor. Truman went to bed thinking he'd probably lost. He woke up president for four more years.

In the second term he forged what became known as the Truman Doctrinc which gave aid to Turkey and Greece and helped bring about one of the largest post-war rebuilding programs ever launched; The Marshall Plan.

June, 1950, Truman's penchant for making swift decisions because the "buck stops here" produced a controversial choice of committing US troops, primarily unprepared headquarter and supply soldiers in Japan and under-strength divisions to battle an invading North Korean Army in South Korea.

He wrote later: There was "complete, almost unspoken acceptance on the part of everyone that whatever had to be done to meet this aggression had to be done. There was no suggestion from anyone that either the United Nations or the United States could back away from it."

An armistice was signed three years later after fighting shifted back and forth across a no-man's land called the DMZ and an estimated 200,000 Chinese troops had joined the battle. While Truman showed the strength to fire popular US General Douglas MacArthur for overstepping his responsibility, the war, which was deceptively called a conflict, hurt Truman's popularity.

He died the day after Christmas, 1972, at 88.

-- From the Presidential Documents Collection of Ben Benson

HARRY S TRUMAN
INDEPENDENCE, MISSOURI
December 30, 1971

Dear Mr. Benson:

I was glad to have your letter and I noted with interest your desire to plan for a career of public service. There can be no higher calling than that of devoting one's self to the public interest.

I would suggest that you acquire a well-rounded education with emphasis on the history of this nation, biographies, political science, economics and law.

It would also help if you would assist those in your neighborhood to get out to vote - and get to know your local and national representatives.

With best wishes for your future,

Sincerely yours,

Harry S. Truman

Mr. Ralph L. Benson
109 West Cottage Street
York, Pennsylvania 17405

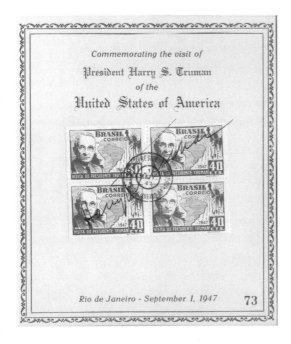

Commemorating the visit of
President Harry S. Truman
of the
United States of America

Rio de Janeiro - September 1, 1947 73

Personal letter detailing how to go into politics.

34th President 1953-1961 Two Terms

Even Franklin Roosevelt might have had trouble marketing a slogan like "I like FDR" during his heyday.

But when Democrats and Republicans, fresh from World War II, heard the phrase "I like Ike," they had to agree it had a positive, comforting ring.

His commanding presence as a general who led the largest armada of the 20th century to victory at Normandy, his ability as a consensus builder in creating the first NATO force and his infectious grin made him appealing to all political parties and the public in 1952. Consequently, when Harry Truman stepped away and Democrats couldn't persuade Ike to join them and chose Sen. Adlai Stevenson instead to head the Democratic ticket, Eisenhower, America's most popular former general, started a political landslide that culminated with a victory margin of 6.6 million in November.

His promises were sketchy but contemporary. He promised to boot the crooks and Communists out of Washington and he said he would "go to Korea" without really offering any plan.

His efforts brought about an uneasy armistice between North and South Korea virtually at a DMZ very close to where the fighting had begun three years earlier. The president, who increased aid to the French in its battle for Indo China, tried to use his mediation to reduce cold war tension with Russia. By 1955, both the US and USSR had hydrogen bombs and world leaders, fearing global destruction that hadn't been seen, met in Geneva, Switzerland. While no binding agreements came from the meeting, the two governments were talking, face to face, and tensions were relaxed.

Two months later, Eisenhower suffered a heart attack and spent the next seven weeks in a Denver hospital while American media tried, in vain, to determine whether Vice President Richard Nixon or Press Secretary James Haggerty was in charge of the White House.

The president survived his attack and ran and won a second term. While his domestic policy in his second four-years was a continuation of New and Fair Deal programs of his predecessors, Ike worked to bring about a balanced budget.

He surprised some and certainly made clear to southern states his determination about education and rights. He dispatched federal troops to Little Rock, AK, September, 1957, to enforce a court order to desegregate the schools and followed with his own order to desegregate the military forces. "There must be no second class citizens in this country," he said.

Meanwhile, he announced an Eisenhower Doctrine aimed at giving aid to any Middle Eastern country threatened by communism.

Before he left office to play more golf and enjoy his Gettysburg farm not far from either the

White House or an FDR retreat in Maryland called Shangri-la which he renamed Camp David where he spent long weekends, he urged the country to continue to maintain an adequate military strength but be mindful of rising military costs that could endanger our way of life.

Dwight Eisenhower died March 28, 1969 at 79.

-- From the Presidential Documents Collection of Ben Benson

```
                    John SD Eisenhower
                    27318 Morris Road
                    Trappe, MD 21673


                              June 5, 1996

Mr. Ralph Benson
21 View Drive
Lexington, VA 24450


Dear Mr. Benson,

     The photos of your paintings were waiting for me
when we returned to Trappe last evening - and handsome
paintings they are!

     Not surprisingly, I think the one of General
Marshall is the best. It has a certain warmth to it
that many other likenesses lack. (The Roosevelt
likeness is more standard.) You obviously interpret
more than paint photographically.

     Many thanks for the trouble and expense you went
to in order to send them to us. We much appreciate
having them.

     I don't have any noticeable wisdom regarding
politics, a fact that has been borne out by the list of
losers I have backed in the past. But my feeling this
year is that the vice-presidential spot is so important
that Dole would be smart to throw the selection out to
the Convention floor, as Stevenson did in 1956. Such a
move would free him from any pressures toward tokenism
and give the delegates the feeling that they are
exercising free choice - which they will not be doing
when voting for the first spot. They have to pick
someone they think can step into the first spot, even
more than usual.

     We'll see.

                         Best regards,

                         John Eisenhower
```

```
              Columbia University
              in the City of New York
                  NEW YORK 27, N Y

              OFFICE OF THE PRESIDENT


                              October 21, 1950


Dear Bob:

Thank you for your heart-warming remem-
brance on my birthday; hereafter, I shall
certainly know where to go for poetry--
made to order.

With warm regard,

                    Sincerely,

                    DDE


Mr. Robert Woodruff
P. O. Box 1734
Atlanta, Ga.
```

Letter written to R. Woodruff, President, Coca Cola, Reference Bob Jones, famous golfer.

35th President 1961-1963

About John Kennedy, historian/publisher David Rubel probably offers the best assessment:

"Historians are hesitant to agree. Some rate Kennedy highly; others, not so well. However, all tend to acknowledge that his assassination, the most pivotal moment in post-war American history, has so transformed our perception of him that the original man --- the living president, not the martyred one --- may be lost forever."

What isn't lost, however, are the turbulent yet vibrant 32 months of the Kennedy White House, called the days of Camelot.

The son of a wealthy, ambitious Massachusetts family, John Kennedy demonstrated the sense of modest, unassuming valor for his exploits as a PT boat skipper in the Pacific, his creativity as an author of a Pulitzer Prize winning book "Profiles of Courage" while recuperating from aggravated wartime injuries and the political acumen and tenacity that led him to a1961 presidential victory; the first Roman Catholic to be elected as well as the youngest (43) to win the office.

Sadly, he was also the youngest president of four murdered while in office, too. It happened in Dallas, Nov. 22, 1963.

But his 16 years in government, which started as a Boston congressman and advanced to senator from Massachusetts brought an excitement that energized not only the young but the whole country, Republican as well as Democrat. An idealist, he said, without illusions, he defeated Vice President Richard Nixon in a narrow contest that was decided by 118,000 votes. In his inaugural he made history by calling for Americans to "Ask not what your country can do for you ... ask what you can do for your country." The vitality of his presidency was measured in days and detailed in Arthur Schlesinger Jr's popular book, "A Thousand Days." Kennedy plunged into perilous waters off America's southern shores approving an infamous Bay of Pigs invasion which left plenty of political debris.

A year later, he had one of the most tense meltdowns with Soviet Union America had seen when Russian missiles suddenly appeared in Cuba. Yet he clearly pledged that the US wanted no conflict. "The United States, as the world knows, will never start a war. We do not want war. This generation of Americans have already had enough ... more than enough ... of war and hate and oppression..." he told a commencement audience at American University months before his death.

He took aggressive measures to advance civil rights and economic systems. Meanwhile, he launched an Alliance for Progress and Peace Corps to built on his human rights initiative. However, he followed his predecessor Dwight Eisenhower by continuing aid and providing US military advisers for a war in Indochina that was built on an illusion of dominos and helping a US ally, the French.

There was also a dark side, Rubel points out. "He didn't treat his wife very well and he could be two-faced. Yet even when those blemishes were revealed ... they never eclipsed the popular memory of his energy, his high spirits and his force of will."

-- From the Presidential Documents Collection of Ben Benson

Office of Gerald R. Ford

On November 22, 1963 President John F. Kennedy was assassinated in Dallas, Texas. It was one of the most tragic and memorable events in the history of the United States.

In the time that has passed since this fateful day, much has been theorized regarding the assassin, Lee Harvey Oswald, and the possibility that he did not act alone in the murder of the President.

In the past thirty years I have witnessed a nation obsessed with this tragedy cling to new theory after new theory, and in turn, forsake the truth.

As a Congressman, I was a member of the Warren Commission appointed to investigate the assassination of President Kennedy.

I examined all the evidence and to this day stand by the Warren Commission Report on the murder of President Kennedy. I believe Lee Harvey Oswald acted Alone in his assassination of the President. I believe that there was a single killer, Lee Harvey Oswald, and that there was no hidden organization in support of him.

These are the only conclusions I can draw, and as the only remaining living member of the Warren Commission, I steadfastly stand by them.

36th President 1963-1969 Two Terms

The eighth vice president in US history who became president because of the sudden death of an incumbent, Lyndon Johnson was, perhaps, one of the most experienced to step into the oval office during a national tragedy.

Look at the famous photo of Johnson being sworn in aboard Air Force One hours after President Kennedy had died and you see a determined, somber yet unflappable leader who recognized the poignancy and power of the moment.

He had spent 24 years in Congress, becoming the youngest Senate Majority Leader at 45 in 1953. A committed FDR New Dealer from Texas when he entered the House in 1937, his persuasive combination of charm, anger and sometimes meanness made him one of the most powerful government leaders of the 20th century.

Johnson, some said, took the term "earthy" and returned it to the "Age of Jackson." Doris Kearns Goodwin, the historian, remembers the coarseness that was done with such nonchalance there was little time to deal with diplomacy. "When he had to go to the bathroom in the middle of a conversation, it was not unusual for him to move the discussion there. Johnson seem delighted as he told me of 'one of the delicate Kennedyites who came into the bathroom ... and then found it utterly impossible to look ... while I sat there on the toilet. You'd think he had never seen those parts of the body before.'"

But Johnson quickly demonstrated his loyalty to JFK by pushing the former president's Civil Rights and Equal Opportunity Acts which "declared war on poverty" as he prepared himself for a second term months away. Surprisingly, he embraced Kennedy's tax cut even if he had doubts about it. Biographer Robert Caro said it best about Johnson's abilities; he had "a rare gift for mobilizing the powers of government to raise up the downtrodden."

The 36th president demonstrated his popularity with the people when he won the 1964 election with the largest margin in American history; more then 15,000,000 votes or 61 percent of those casting ballots.

Johnson unveiled his "Great Society" program in January, 1965. The program attacked problems the way a health department battles a virus. His Great Society, he claimed, would aid education, attack disease, build Medicare, deal with urban renewal, beautification, conservation, renovate depressed regions of the country, launch a war on poverty, go after crime and delinquency and make voting the right of eligible citizens. That was the beginning. On a global front, Johnson championed space exploration programs, telling the three astronauts on the successful moon orbit in December, 1968, "You've taken ... all of us, all over the world, into a new era."

Yet the nation was troubled by hot summers that erupted in rioting in Black ghettos from coast to coast. Johnson used all of his considerable political influence against segregation but solutions were still just beyond his grasp.

Vietnam, of course, was even more difficult because Johnson had continued Eisenhower and Kennedy's path in using military advisers and military aid to bolster weak and corrupt governments in Southeast Asia. Probably the worst moment in the Johnson presidency was the Tonkin Gulf Resolution of 1964 which, some believe, was engineered by the White House and gave the president "nearly unlimited power to use military force in Vietnam without a formal declaration of war." While the US insisted it did not want to widen the war, the Johnson Administration escalated US military force from 3,500 Marines to more than 500,000 armed forces in four years.

The policy and the failure to bring the desired results in Southeast Asia caused Johnson to withdraw from the presidential race in 1968. When he left the White House, peace talks were underway. However, Lyndon Johnson didn't get to see what he had hoped; a settlement of the war. He suffered a heart attack on January 22, 1973, at his Texas ranch and died at 65.

-- From the Presidential Documents Collection of Ben Benson

This is the Grand Entrance — I always think of it in connection with State dinners and the arrival of the guests of honor — Kings, Presidents, Prime Ministers — Lady Bird Johnson

LYNDON B. JOHNSON
TEXAS

REC'D JUN 20 1953
File

United States Senate
Office of the Minority Leader
Washington, D. C.

June 18, 1953

Dear Mr. President:

The enclosed very warm invitation comes from R. L. Thornton, President of the State Fair of Texas, who hopes that you can attend the State Fair in Dallas after your scheduled meeting with the President of Mexico at the dedication of Falcon Dam in October.

We know how much it would mean to Mr. Thornton and to Texans if you could arrange to drop by the State Fair in October, and are very glad to join with Mr. Thornton and the State Fair of Dallas in extending this invitation to you and urging your acceptance.

Sincerely

Lyndon B. Johnson

Price Daniel

The Honorable
The President
Washington

copy to Senator Daniel

Letter written to President Eisenhower.

37th President 1969-1974 Two Terms

For a young man from a poor Quaker family, Richard Nixon's life was shaped by an anger that gave him an inner strength of conviction and, at the same time, destroyed much of the legacy he hoped so much he would leave for posterity.

America's 37th president, like many of his predecessors, served as an officer (Navy) in World War II, although not in combat. He returned home not to put up a shingle a a lawyer from the prestigious Duke University Law School but to get elected to Congress in 1946. Four years later, he became a US Senator from California.

He was in the right place at the right time when popular WWII hero, Gen.Dwight Eisenhower ran for president on the Republican ticket in 1952. At 39, Nixon offered a good balance in age with the 60-year-old Ike. However, Nixon encountered the first of the major gaffs that pursued him through his political career.

When it was discovered that he may have accepted questionable contributions he was forced to make a nationally televised address of contrition, called the "Checkers" speech, to save his candidacy. Eisenhower's ill health and Nixon's ambition gave him a major role during the 1950's. Nixon, however, lost a close race for the presidency in 1960 to another WWII Navy veteran, Sen.John F. Kennedy. Several years later in a campaign for the governorship for California, Nixon's self-control became a media issue when he told reporters "You won't have Nixon to kick around anymore because ... this is my last press conference." But he was back six years later more determined than ever, some believe. And his accomplishments during the next five years were very impressive his critics concede. He brought forward revenue sharing, new anti-crime measures, a broad environmental program and, on his watch, American astronauts Neal Armstrong and Edwin "Buzz" Aldrin Jr. sent back word from the moon that Apollo II had landed and man had taken "one small step ... one giant leap for mankind."

In foreign affairs, Nixon engineered major advances that were equal if not more impressive. He accelerated a so-called "secret plan" to bring about an accord with North Vietnam to end the fighting in Southeast Asia although it left American forces scrambling to leave on helicopters from an embattled embassy in Saigon.

His summit meetings with Leonid Brezhnev of Russia limited strategic nuclear weapons. It was an illusive prize that escaped other US presidents during the Cold War.

He appeared to reverse his position as an ardent anti Communist when he visited China in early 1972 and opened the doors of a country long closed to the western world.

Consequently, his re-election against liberal Democrat Sen. George McGovern the same year was one of the largest landslides on record.

Twenty-four months later, a scandal that surfaced on the pages of the Washington Post because of the work of two enterprising reporters called "Watergate" involving a break-in at the Democratic National

Committees eroded Nixon's popularity, political strength and reputation . Cover up attempts which later convicted some of his administration members, forced the president to resign or face the reality of the impeachment of a sitting president. On Aug. 9, 1974, an exhausted and crying Nixon family boarded a military helicopter on the South Lawn for its final departure from the White House.

In his later years, Nixon regained status as an elder statesman thanks to his writings and speeches on public life and foreign policy.

What was the most requested photo of the Nixon years says the National Archives? It wasn't his departure or his lonely vigils at Camp David in the Catoctin Mountains. It was a photo taken Dec. 21, 1970, of Elvis Presley and Nixon at the White House after Presley had written a 6-page letter to the president to be named a "federal agent at large" in the Bureau of Narcotics and Dangerous Drugs.

Richard Nixon died April 22, 1994, at 81.

-- From the Presidential Documents Collection of Ben Benson

PETER W. RODINO, JR.
10th District, New Jersey

CHAIRMAN
COMMITTEE ON THE JUDICIARY

Congress of the United States
House of Representatives
Washington, D.C. 20515

DISTRICT OFFICE:
FEDERAL BUILDING
970 BROAD STREET
NEWARK, NEW JERSEY 07102
TELEPHONE: 645-3213

May 9, 1975

Mr. Ralph L. Benson
21 Tallmadge Avenue
Chatham, New Jersey 07928

Dear Mr. Benson:

Mr. Tony Suriano of my District Office has forwarded to me your letter of May 2. I certainly appreciate knowing of your support and I hope to continue to merit your confidence.

One of the most satisfying aspects of the "Watergate affair" was the fact that all 38 Members of the House Judiciary Committee accepted their responsibility and realized that their actions were concerned not with an individual but with a system of Constitutional government.

I am certainly proud to have been a part of these historic proceedings.

Thank you for writing to me.

Kind regards.

Sincerely,

PETER W. RODINO, JR.
M. C.

PWR/gd

United States Senate
COMMITTEE ON FOREIGN RELATIONS
WASHINGTON, D.C. 20510

J. W. FULBRIGHT, ARK., CHAIRMAN

JOHN SPARKMAN, ALA.   GEORGE D. AIKEN, VT.
MIKE MANSFIELD, MONT.   CLIFFORD P. CASE, N.J.
FRANK CHURCH, IDAHO   JACOB K. JAVITS, N.Y.
STUART SYMINGTON, MO.   HUGH SCOTT, PA.
CLAIBORNE PELL, R.I.   JAMES B. PEARSON, KANS.
GALE W. McGEE, WYO.   CHARLES H. PERCY, ILL.
EDMUND S. MUSKIE, MAINE   ROBERT P. GRIFFIN, MICH.
GEORGE McGOVERN, S.DAK.
HUBERT H. HUMPHREY, MINN.

PAT M. HOLT, CHIEF OF STAFF
ARTHUR M. KUHL, CHIEF CLERK

June 3, 1974

Dear Mr. Benson:

Many thanks for your recent letter. The depth of your concern over the discontent and frustration shared by so many Americans these days is obvious. I am confident that you do care and will continue working to return this nation to the ideals upon which it was founded.

If I have remained somewhat out of the limelight in regard to the disclosure of diminishing morality at the highest levels of American government, it has been because I did not wish to seem vindictive. During the 1972 campaign, I warned Americans repeatedly of the corrupt Nixon Administration and the meaning of Watergate. But after the election, I felt it was time for others to take that vocal lead.

However, as you can see by the enclosed speech, long before now I recognized the need to resolve the questions surrounding the presidency and to restore confidence in our national leadership. And I am confident that this goal will be reached and that Congress will meet its historic obligation with care and integrity.

With every good wish, I am

Sincerely yours,

George McGovern

Ralph L. Benson
21 Tallmadge Ave.
Chatham, NJ 07928

Enclosure

RICHARD NIXON

September 29, 1980

Dear Mr. Benson:

This is just a note to express my deep appreciation for your writing as you did with regard to The Real War.

I hope it may provide some useful guidance for our policy makers in the future.

Sincerely,

Richard Nixon

Mr. Ralph L. Benson
21 Tallmadge Avenue
Chatham, New Jersey 07928

The Speaker's Rooms
U.S. House of Representatives
Washington, D.C. 20515

June 16, 1976

Mr. Ralph L. Benson
21 Tallmadge Avenue
Chatham, New Jersey 07928

Dear Mr. Benson:

Thank you for your letter. I appreciate very much your kind words. The American spirit which we celebrate in commemorating our 200th birthday was also present when the Constitution of our country was born. The Constitution has been my guiding light during 30 years in Congress. It has reaffirmed my belief that ours is a government of laws and not of men.

I feel a special attachment to the Constitution as I presided over the House of Representatives at a time when the Constitution was severely tested. Less than three years ago, a President and a Vice President resigned for the first time in our history. As a result, I was twice one heartbeat away from the Presidency. After implementation of the 25th Amendment, this nation had both an appointed President and an appointed Vice President and today I remain the highest elected official in the government. Had the 25th Amendment not been ratified, I, as a member of the Democratic Party, would have become President of the United States less than two years after the American people gave a Republican President the largest majority vote in history.

After participating in this dramatic but smooth transition at a divisive and traumatic time in our history, my steadfast faith in the Constitution and the American people is strengthened immeasurably. Representative government works; the Constitution of the United States lives.

Sincerely,

Carl Albert
The Speaker

CA/fst

October 29, 1973

Dear Mr. Benson:

Your support and encouragement meant a great deal to me.

I can only reaffirm my innocence to you and hope, in this complex and confusing situation, that you will try to understand that I believe the actions I have taken are in the best interest of the Nation.

Sincerely,

[signature]

September 2, 1973

Dear Mr. Benson:

Your most thoughtful note was deeply appreciated.

As I said at the hearings, I fully expect the truth to be known eventually -- and when it is, it will be abundantly clear that neither our great President nor I had any involvement in or knowledge of wrongdoing.

In the meantime, it is most heart-warming to know of your support.

Thank you very much for your kind words -- and my very best wishes to you and your family.

Sincerely,

Bob Haldeman

H. R. Haldeman

Mr. R. L. Benson
21 Tallmadge Avenue
Chatham, New Jersey

Gerald R. Ford

Fate has terrible power. You cannot escape it by wealth or war. No fort will keep it out, no ships outrun it.

-- *Sophocles, Antigone*

Gerald Ford encountered fate not once but twice in less than a year and both experiences were tests of the country's checks and balances and a government in crisis.

A popular Michigan congressman during his 25 years in the House of Representatives, he was better known for his integrity and openness than his legislation. Ford described himself as a "moderate on domestic issues, a conservative in fiscal affairs and a dyed-in-the-wool internationalist."

He was the choice of congressional leaders and President Nixon for vice president when bribery charges forced Spiro Agnew to vacate the office in December, 1973. Ironically, it was Gerald Ford who had helped enact the 25th Amendment which prescribed the procedure for filling vice presidential vacancies years earlier.

Eight months later, fate intervened again when on Aug. 9, 1974, the former Republican Minority Leader was sworn in as president hours after Nixon resigned. He was the first president in US history to take the oval office without winning a national election. The task he faced was of major proportion for the individual and the nation, Democrats and Republicans agreed. After he repeated the oath he recognized the enormity of the challenges he faced. "I assume the Presidency under extraordinary circumstances ... This is an hour of history that troubles our minds and hurts our hearts."

That was probably and understatement considering the upheaval the country was enduring. Inflation had to be dealt with right away, as did unemployment. The economy was depressed and had to be revived and there was a threatening energy shortage. And the world certainly wasn't a safe place either.

Ford acted to reduce government intervention as the way to solve problems but in 30 days after he took office he surprised Republicans and Democrats by announcing that he had granted Nixon an unconditional pardon for any crimes he might have committed as president. The pardon was criticized although Ford believed it was necessary to avoid what he sincerely believed would be "ugly passions" if the former president was put on trial.

Overseas, Ford acted to show US power and prestige in Southeast Asia and in trying to prevent a war in the Middle East. The president took his message abroad in November, 1974, by visiting Japan, South Korea and the Soviet Union where he continued Nixon's policy of reducing the threat of nuclear war by reaching a tentative agreement with Leonid Brezhnev to reduce strategic offensive weapons.

The 38th president had used his personal diplomacy to work with Congress during his abbreviated term but Republican Ronald Reagan's attacks on his administration's foreign policy took its toll as the country prepared for another election. In his first formal bid for the office, Ford lost to Georgia Gov. Jimmy Carter. But even his opponent had words of praise for Ford and his 36 month effort to bind a divided country. Said President-elect Carter on his inaugural day in 1977: "For myself and our Nation, I want to thank my predecessor for all he has done to heal our land." There were many who agreed.

-- From the Presidential Documents Collection of Ben Benson

Very Rare: Use of Gerald Ford's middle name Rudolph

There were few presidential candidates whose aspirations were higher. There have been few times in US history when the country wanted someone not tied to partisan politics than it did in the 1976 election.

Jimmy Carter, a former naval officer in the submarine service and independent young Georgia governor, seemed to meet those requirements. Clearly an outsider and an ordinary guy, he began campaigning 24 months early championing popular issues like ecology, government efficiency and the removal of racial walls. He swept the Democratic National convention on the first ballot and teamed with Sen. Walter Mondale of Minnesota to defeat Republican Gerald Ford.

While his moralistic attitude and carping irritated a number in both parties and over four years took its toll on his image, Carter worked long days and nights to make necessary changes. In four years, for example, he reduced the budget deficit and helped patch together an economy that grew 8 million jobs. He attacked energy as a national crisis and foreign imports rose days after he took office. He called it "the moral equivalent of war" and urged conservation and waste reduction among a number of ways to establish a national energy program.

He expanded the national park system, created a Department of Education, energized the Social Security System, appointed a large number of women, Blacks, Hispanics to government jobs, deregulated the airline and banking industries and lifted price controls on oil.

In world affairs, Carter brought old school Middle East leaders Anwar el-Sadat of Egypt and Menachem Begin of Israel together for the first of country-to country meetings. The first one produced the Camp David Agreement of 1978. Following up on Nixon and Ford efforts with the Soviet Union, Carter completed a SALT II treaty with Russia and established a better relationship with China. In the Americas, he brought about ratification of the Panama Canal Treaties.

His accomplishments when one looks back were very significant but he faced setbacks in the last months of his tenure that damaged his presidency. Soviet invasion of Afghanistan suspended the SALT II ratification. Political unrest in Iran blew up on the president's watch in 1979 when militants seized 52 Americans from the US Embassy in Tehran leaving Carter little room to negotiate or exert political pressure. Eight US Marines were killed in a failed rescue attempt later.

Consequently, his last 14 months were overtaken by the 444-day ordeal of innocent hostages and a stagnated and inflated economy. To add personal injury to the president,

Iran, calling the United States "The Great Satan," released the hostages as President-elect Ronald Reagan took office and Carter left.

For a man with high aspirations it was another defeat ... yet to some it didn't set aside the successes, either.

"All these issues were tough, they were controversial, very few of them had any political upside to them. But he did'em, because they were right," former Carter Chief of Staff Hamilton Jordan said in retrospect.

-- From the Presidential Documents Collection of Ben Benson

THE WHITE HOUSE
WASHINGTON

7-2-80

To Ralph Benson
    Mr. Kirbo sent me your note.
    Thank you for the good advice and offer of support. Keeping our nation at peace, strong & united will indeed be a challenge to us all, & the campaign will be a good forum for debating these issues.

                    Jimmy C.

DEPARTMENT OF STATE
Washington, D.C. 20520

December 6, 1979

Mr. Ralph Benson
21 Tallmadge Avenue
Chatham, New Jersey 07928

Dear Mr. Benson:

Thank you for your communication to President Carter concerning the grave situation in Iran.

For that government to applaud mob violence and terrorism, and actually to support and in effect participate in the taking and the holding of hostages is unprecedented in human history. Nations and people from around the world have voiced their condemnation of Iran and have joined us in calling for the release of the hostages.

We hold the Government of Iran responsible for the well-being and the safe return of every single hostage. We are deeply concerned about the inhuman and degrading conditions imposed on them, and we will not rest nor deviate from our efforts until every single American has been freed.

We hope this can be achieved through the peaceful exercise of diplomacy and international law, which is preferable to the other remedies available to the United States. As the President has said, "the Government of Iran must recognize the gravity of the situation which it has, itself, created and the grave consequences which will result if harm comes to any of the hostages."

The Administration welcomes and appreciates the restraint that has been shown by the American people. We must continue to exhibit such constraint despite the intensity of our emotions. The lives of our people in Iran are at stake.

Sincerely,

Hodding Carter III
Assistant Secretary
for Public Affairs and
Department Spokesman

40th President 1981-1989 Two Terms

If there was a president most Americans felt comfortable with it was Ronald Reagan. Democrats and Republicans alike were as ready in the 1980s for Dutch Reagan, a former California governor who spent two decades making 53 movies including some B films like Bedtime for Bonzo and an early version of Law and Order, as they were in the 1950s for WWII hero General Dwight Eisenhower.

But it wasn't simply Hollywood credentials or his California political experience that gave Reagan appeal. Americans were troubled about their insecurity. There was double digit inflation and a recession that months earlier had cut real output by more than 9 percent. Housing starts had dropped 33 percent.

Worse, within days after taking office a young assassin tried to kill the president. Fortunately, the 70-year-old Reagan recovered quickly and by Fall had requested a $13 billion cut for 1982. An economic plan called "Reaganomics" was underway.

Though he was criticized for his lack of economic understanding of financial needs during precarious times Reagan skillfully dealt with Congress to bring about economic growth, curb inflation, increase employment and bolster the national defense. He won high marks for appointing the first woman, Sandra Day O'Connor of Arizona, to the Supreme Court. However, a year later there were more problems internationally than answers for the Reagan Administration. The president ordered an invasion of Grenada to combat a Cuban threat to take over the island. Close ties between Havana and the Caribbean island and the construction of a 10,000 foot runway which Washington suggested could handle Soviet and Cuban fights caused growing concern. Just two days before the invasion by US Marines and Army Rangers, marines were attacked in Lebanon and 241 were killed. But the economy did improve and Reagan, still popular with the people, was re-elected in 1984 in a landslide victory over Walter Mondale and Geraldine Ferraro.

Second terms, though, can be difficult for popular presidents and Reagan found truth in the statement. The budget deficit grew and the president and Congress fought over the government priorities; defense or domestic matters. A Nicaraguan Contra scandal which was linked to the White House through covert monies given to guerrilla fighters Reagan claimed were the "moral equal to our Founding Fathers" backfired and Congress refused to support military funding. The continuation of the congressional investigation in later months was thought to have damaged the Republicans in the midterm elections.

The president, however, continued to be popular with Americans because he took responsibility while claiming he had no knowledge of the details. A passive leader as compared to Carter and others, Reagan was known to delegate responsibilities to aides which added veracity to his explanation.

Yet it was Reagan who may have been the first president of the latter part of the 20th century to declare war on international terrorism. In April 1986, after determining that Syria was responsible for the death of a US soldier in a West Berlin nightclub bombing, Reagan dispatched a US air strike to attack Muammar Qadoffi's Tripoli headquarters. The unilateral action brought the nation together but incensed the NATO alliance.

As his tenure entered the final months, he met with Soviet leader Mikhail Gorbachev in Moscow in May, 1988, to sign an agreement on verification inspections between the two countries but irritated the Russians by encouraging more civil and religious liberties.

Without doubt, Reagan's eight years brought surprising domestic achievements; sharp cuts in income tax rates, the creation of economic growth without inflation and the reduction of unemployment. At the same time, the "Reagan Revolution" failed to bring achievements on abortion and school prayer.

-- From the Presidential Documents Collection of Ben Benson

A sample of what I'd do at Camp David when we spent a weekend there.

To
Ralph Benson
Best Wishes
Nancy Reagan

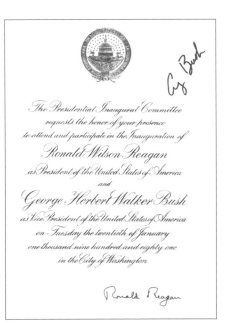

Cy Bush

The Presidential Inaugural Committee
requests the honor of your presence
to attend and participate in the Inauguration of

Ronald Wilson Reagan

as President of the United States of America
and

George Herbert Walker Bush

as Vice President of the United States of America
on Tuesday the twentieth of January
one thousand nine hundred and eighty one
in the City of Washington

Ronald Reagan

THE WHITE HOUSE
WASHINGTON

September 7, 1983

Dear Mr. Benson:

Your letter to the President regarding the allegations that the 1980 Reagan/Bush campaign received certain briefing materials from the Carter campaign has been referred to me for response.

I can assure you that the President has but one motive in this matter -- to get to the truth. To that end, as I trust you know from recent press accounts, he has instructed that any former members of the Reagan/Bush campaign staff or members of the White House staff with information or documents relating to the allegations provide such information directly to the Office of the Attorney General in Washington, D. C. Further, he instructed me to notify the FBI that everyone in the Administration, including himself, is available for questioning.

Uopn completion of the FBI's investigation, the President will take whatever action is appropriate.

Thank you taking the time to share with us your views on this subject and for your kind words in support of the President.

Sincerely,

Fred F. Fielding
Counsel to the President

Mr. Ralph L. Benson
21 Tallmadge Avenue
Chatham, New Jersey 07928

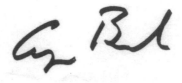

Without a doubt, George Herbert Walker Bush was well connected with the White House and Washington politics long before he took the oath as president.

He was a distant relative by birth to four presidents (Franklin Pierce, Theodore Roosevelt, Abraham Lincoln and Gerald Ford) and his father, Senator Prescott Bush, spent 11 years representing the state of Connecticut.

While he grew up in privileged surroundings in New England, he, like others of his generation, enlisted in the military in the early part of World War II the day he turned 18. He entered the Navy a Seaman 2nd class and, within a year, was the youngest pilot flying torpedo bombers. Upon completing three years of combat duty, he was awarded medals for courageous service. After the war, he moved his young family to Texas and started work in the oil fields as a supply salesman. At 30, he was cofounder of this third oil development company. Elected twice to the House of Representatives from Houston, he lost a Senate bid in 1970. A year later, he was named Ambassador to the United Nations. He spent the rest of the decade serving as chairman of the Republican National Committee and as director of the Central Intelligence Agency.

Ronald Reagan chose Bush as his president in 1981. His service to his country and to Reagan made him American's choice for president in 1988 when he became the first sitting vice president in 150 years to be elected president. He defeated Democrat Gov. Michael Dukakis of Massachusetts with a pledge of "no new taxes."

Though criticized in the early days of his tenure for a lack of leadership and a stalemate over getting appointees approved, Bush conducted major arms control summits with Russia, ordered the invasion of Panama to protect US citizens and overthrow Gen. Manuel Noreiga's corrupt regime.

His popularity in the Oval Office reached its highest when he brought together a coalition of 30 countries to oppose Iraq's invasion of Kuwait and defeat Saddam Hussein in Operation Desert Storm.

At home, he helped bring about a sweeping new program to assist the disabled with the Americans With Disabilities Act and a revised version of the Clean Air Act.

However, persistently high unemployment and a deepening economic recession and a struggle in 1992 with a three-way presidential campaign involving independent Ross Perot and Democrat Bill Clinton took its toll on Bush's campaign to continue.

He became the 10th incumbent to lose.

-- From the Presidential Documents Collection of Ben Benson

THE WHITE HOUSE

WASHINGTON

April 9, 1991

Dear Mr. Benson:

Thank you for your message about the United States
efforts in the Persian Gulf region. This was not a
war we wanted, but there are times in the life of our
country when we confront principles worth fighting
for; this was one such time.

The cooperation of the community of nations in
stopping Saddam Hussein's ruthless aggression and
in liberating Kuwait is unprecedented. Certainly I
am pleased that the war ended so quickly and that
there were far fewer casualties than had been widely
predicted. Operation Desert Storm's success belongs
to our courageous troops. We are all tremendously
proud of them, and I am delighted that they are
coming home to the hero's welcome that they deserve.

As we assume our responsibility as a catalyst
for peace and stability in the Middle East region,
we will not forget those who gave their lives for
this just cause, those who lost loved ones, or those
innocent people who have suffered as a result of this
conflict. I ask for your prayers for all those thus
affected and for continued blessings on our great
Nation.

Sincerely,

George Bush

**GEORGE BUSH PRESIDENTIAL LIBRARY
DEDICATION DAY TOUR OF MUSEUM**
Thursday, November 6, 1997
12:30pm-5:30pm

This ticket admits one

*G Bush
Barbara Bush*

GEORGE BUSH

*Dear Ralph,
All 3 of us were
glad to sign this
cover (attached)
Good luck
G Bush*

*Hope your wife
feels well -
Barbara*

He made a momentous decision about a career after a White House Rose Garden visit as a delegate to Boys' Nation.

In a chance meeting with President John F. Kennedy, William Clinton decided to put his saxophone and his dream of becoming a professional musician away. It wasn't easy. He was considered one of the best players in the state.

He decided, instead, to embark on a life in public service.

Opinions vary on whether he made the right decision but the truth is he didn't give up music for his "day job" either. He took his "ax" to the White House and played a few "gigs" whenever invited to "sit in".

So did Harry Truman and Richard Nixon, of course.

Bill Clinton's' Administration, Republicans reluctantly concede and Democrats speak proudly about, made progress with economic and social concerns. His administration had the lowest unemployment rate in years, the lowest inflation in 30 years, the highest home ownership in US history, reduced welfare numbers and it brought a drop in the crime rate, too.

And it happened with the youngest elected president (47) in America's history whose previous experience was two terms as the youngest governor of the State of Arkansas. He entered the presidential race in 1992 with a number of personal issues that stalked him throughout his tenure in office. He was opposed to the Vietnam War and was attacked by veterans and members of both parties for avoiding a military obligation. He was also charged with infidelity with not one but several women. A real estate deal, later labeled Whitewater, subjected Clinton and his wife Hillary to scrutiny about their participation. While charges of fraud and conspiracy were filed against a number of people and several went to jail, the Clintons were never accused of wrongdoing.

Politically, Clinton had to deal major matters days after he was sworn in. A pledge he had made to allow homosexuals to serve in the military openly was attacked and he had to compromise with a confusing but accepted position called "don't ask, don't tell."

1994 proved to be even more turbulent. A Republican Congress and the president battled over a health care reform plan, managed by Hillary, as well as welfare reform and crime prevention. All proposals failed but he crafted successful legislation with Congress to bring about the North American Free Trade Agreement (NAFTA) and Global Agreement on Tariffs and Trade (GATT). He also worked with Congress to obtain deficit reduction, abortion counseling and a waiting period for purchasing a handgun (The Brady Bill).

His trials and tribulations became an international scandal when he was accused of an amorous relationship with a White House intern in 1998. Clinton became the second US president to be impeached by the House. Like Andrew Johnson 130 years earlier he was tried in the Senate and found not guilty. He apologized to the country for his actions.

-- From the Presidential Documents Collection of Ben Benson

THE WHITE HOUSE

WASHINGTON

April 9, 1997

<u>PERSONAL</u>

Mr. Ralph Benson
36 Rockport Road
New Hartford, New York   13413

Dear Ralph:

    Thanks for the print, which Senator Moynihan forwarded to me. I appreciate your kindness in sending another copy. My presidential library is slated to be established in Little Rock, Arkansas.

    You have my best wishes.

Sincerely,

Bill Clinton

106TH CONGRESS—FIRST SESSION

United States Senate

Impeachment Trial of the
PRESIDENT OF THE UNITED STATES

DATE FEB 0 6 1999

ADMIT BEARER TO THE SENATE GALLERY

Sergeant at Arms United States Senate

43rd President, 2001-2005

The first president of the 21st Century to face the challenge of rampant international terrorism, George W. Bush found himself mobilizing a grieving and shocked nation following the horrendous attack Sept. 11, 2001, on New York City's World Trade Center. It left thousands dead and a cavernous hole of destruction in one of the world's major cities.

"The pictures of airplanes flying into buildings, fires burning, huge structures collapsing, have created disbelief, terrible sadness and a great, unyielding anger," the president told an anguished nation hours after the assault on American soil. "These acts of mass murder were intended to frighten our nation into chaos and retreat. But they have failed; our country is strong ... America was targeted for attack because we're the brightest beacon and opportunity for the world. And no one will keep that light from shining ..."

Like his predecessor, Bush was also an ex-governor (Texas) who had been successful in working both sides of the aisle. However, he described himself as a "compassionate conservative."

The first president not just to throw out the first pitch but to own a professional baseball team -- Texas Rangers (co-owner) -- he entered office by a very narrow electoral margin after losing the popular election to Clinton Vice President, Al Gore. It took five weeks after the election for the US Supreme Court to determine that Bush had won the electoral votes to become the president.

Like his father, George W. went to Yale then entered the oil business in Texas. In his 2001 State of the Union address, Bush identified what he considered to be an "Axis of Evil" in the world which he believed had to be addressed. The phrase described Iran, Iraq and North Korea. Several years later, the president mounted an international campaign to disarm Saddam Hussein. Earlier, he had launched a multi-faceted attack in Afghanistan to remove the Taliban and its leader Osama Bin Laden.

His campaign against Iraq accused the country of having weapons of mass destruction which posed a threat to the US and world security. In 2003, the US and British forces invaded Iraq and occupied the country.

The battle against el Quada and elements of the Taliban and irregular forces in Iraq continue today.

--- *From the Presidential Documents Collection of Ben Benson*

GEORGE W. BUSH
GOVERNOR

October 5, 1998

Mr. Ralph Benson
36 Rockport Road
New Hartford, New York 13413

Dear Ralph:

I appreciate so very much your thoughtful letter concerning my
hesitancy to run for the Presidency. I expressed concern about the
current status in Washington. I did so not out of fear of scrutiny on my
background, but out of concern for my young girls and my wife, who I
adore more than anything.

However, I have yet to make up my mind one way or the other. I will
do so next spring. Should I decide to run, I would value your support.

I appreciate your considerate letter.

Sincerely yours,

George W. Bush

Ben Benson

Going back to early childhood, I always had an interest in art and history. At 7, for example, I remembered creating birthday cards for my family. For years, I sketched and painted for my own amusement.

One of my earliest school memories was in the fourth grade. The class was given a homework assignment to do a report on China. Our teacher encouraged us to obtain source material from the library. We were told of the importance of learning about another country's culture. Like my classmates, I suppose, I put off this "major" task until the last moment. To make up for a lack of content, I did what I liked to do; I drew a creative cover which portrayed a Chinese coolie balancing bamboo baskets on hunched shoulders. The cover, I thought, would certainly make up for the lack of pages of written words.

When she gave back the projects, my teacher looked at me with an amused expression. "Read the comments," she said. I got an "A" for artwork and a "C" - for content with the postscript, "nice try but next time spend more time on the subject matter." It was a lesson I didn't forget.

Growing up during the days of President Franklin D. Roosevelt, I developed a keen interest in history and the presidency. During this time, of course, there was no 24-hour Cable News ... consequently, the president and the White House didn't get as much exposure. You heard him on the radio, saw him if you were a movie-goer watching Pathe Newsreel between the feature films and, of course, in the newspapers. Because Roosevelt was such a dynamic personality, he left a lasting impression. I still feel it today.

In college, I took up art as a minor to go along with a business major.

When I stepped from college to a career, I realized it would be extremely difficult to make a living as an artist. However, I never lost my interest in art, history and politics. During the 1960 presidential campaign between John F. Kennedy and Richard Nixon, I began visiting museums and examining presidential collections. It piqued my interest. After the election, I wrote to Evelyn Lincoln, President Kennedy's personal secretary and told her how impressed I was with the administration's domestic and world policies. A few weeks later, I received a personally inscribed and signed photograph of the President. That was my very first presidential piece and the beginning of my quest of more than 40 years.

As I prepared my own collection, I noted that those I had seen had documents that were framed with photographs or black and white prints obtained from the Bureau of Engraving in Washington, DC. The more collections I saw the more identical photos and prints I found so I decided that I could create my own portraits to frame the original documents I collected.

I experimented with colored wax pencils and oils before developing my own technique. Using wax pencils, layering and a wax base, I gave my portraits a three-dimensional appearance.

To ensure an appropriate approach, I read biographies of each president to capture personality, strength and character.

Many of the documents in this collection were obtained without cost by writing directly to the sitting or ex-president, his aides and or staff. To date, I have collected authentic personal correspondence from nine presidents. And I've expanded, too. I collect vice presidents, first ladies and famous politicians of each era.

Like others, I also obtain documents from auctions, trading with fellow collectors and from the estates of deceased politicians.

Technology, of course, affects all of us who collect. One of the major obstacles is the increased use of the autopen which mechanically signs or stamps signatures. The value of such collecting?

It's an on-going learning experience. FDR continued to collect and work on his stamp collection during the dark days of World War II and the most feverish periods of his campaigns. Similarly, to be able to hold a paper that Washington, Jefferson, Lincoln, Roosevelt or others put worlds to is equally thrilling to me.

I sincerely believe that collectors are the care-keepers of our history. It is their goal to preserve and protect that provides a repository of our nation's history for future generations.

Jack Behrens

My fascination with American history was reinforced every day I drove to work in my hometown of Lancaster, Oh. I passed the red bricked residence of William Tecumseh Sherman and I'd make a mental note to visit it. I joined the area's Civil War Roundtable which met in various members' homes but never at the Sherman house. My wife and I, in fact, took a leisurely trip to visit Civil War sites in four states because of my curiosity. Regrettably, like so many of us ... I never got to the Sherman home while I lived in Ohio. It was always something I was going to do "tomorrow."

American history, however, has been my life and work since my graduate school days at Pennsylvania State University where a former State Department consultant and history professor, Phillip Klein, opened vistas of the past that intrigued me.

My master's thesis, for example, was the first to be done as a joint journalism/American history project and the first to explore the murky history of newspaper secrecy violations of the United States Senate. Some of my journalism professors weren't enthusiastic. Philip Klein was. It lead to some interesting arguments about major academic papers and their value.

Forty-seven years later, my musty thesis was a part of the research for this book as it has been for a number of others along the way.

While I've been employed and freelanced as a writer, reporter and editor for more than 30 periodicals and newspapers and authored or edited 17 books, the historical thread stitches together my life and work.

And along the way, I got the chance to see the federal government from the inside as an administrative aide to a democratic Ohio congressman in 1965 and experience the early days of exciting change that President Lyndon Johnson brought with the Great Society. Later, I spent a day working for national media listening to the great communicator, President Ronald Reagan, Secretary of State James Baker and others at the White House outlining the tax policies that brought economic adjustments to America. Earlier, I covered the continuing talks on mundane and sometimes trivia issues at a place called Panmunjom and talked shop with a man writing an epic story during his layover on Okinawa, James Michener. It was a part of my very American experience.

Columbia Scholastic Press Association not long ago rewarded me with a Gold Key recognition for my 35-year effort to build a college press history which continues today as the Student Press Archives in the Utica College, NY Frank E. Gannett Library. It's the only repository of its kind about student press media.

The Virginia Gazette, Journalism History, Editor & Publisher, Mankind and other magazines published my findings about breaches of secrecy in colonial governing chambers entitled "Virginia's Pentagon papers: The Jamestown Acts of 1682." Harvard's Neiman Reports honored me for my research and written account of the investigation of the New York Herald in 1848 as it compared to 20th century secrecy provisions.

My own exploits as a teenage drummer playing in regional big bands and my study of the history of America's ballrooms and the swing era produced my 16th book and a different kind of cultural history not long ago entitled *The Big Band Days: A Memoir and Source Book* (1st Books Library/2003).

Histories of colleges and personalities have consumed hours, days, weeks and months of my career as a writer and editor and will continue to do so because there is so much to be learned from others whether it be their mistakes or successes ... or both. It's the stuff life is made of, I've discovered.

My collaboration with Ben Benson and the Oneida County Historical Society to convey the fascinating stories and intimate memoranda of America's 43 presidents has been another milestone for me. It provides an intimate view of the ambition, frailty and humanity of men who controlled the destiny of the world's most powerful country.

I do hope you enjoy what we've provided on these pages.

Presidential Profile Book Bibliography

Agel, Jerome B, We, The People, Barnes & Noble, 1997

Behrens, John C., Newspaper Violations of United States Senate Secrecy
    Injunctions, 1844 and 1848, master's thesis, the Pennsylvania State University, 1956

Bowers, Claude G. Jefferson in Power, Houghton Mifflin 1967

Burns, James MacGregor, Roosevelt: The Soldier of Freedom, 1940-1945 Harcourt,
Brace, Jovanovich, 1970

Buchanan, A. Russell, The United States and World War II (Vol. I) Harper Torchbook, 1964

Buchanan, A.Russell, The United States and World War II (Vol. II) Harper Torchbook, 1964

Cannon, Lou, Reagan, G.P. Putnam's Sons, 1982

Documents of American History, Henry Steele Commager, ed, Appleton Century Crofts,
1968

Dwight D. Eisenhower, Mandate for Change, 1953-1956, New American Library, 1963

Franklin D. Roosevelt: Age of Action, Alfred B. Rollins, Jr. ed., Dell, 1960

Hersh, Seymour M., The Dark Side of Camelot, Little Brown 1997

Inaugural Addresses, Presidents of the United States, 1789-1969
    US Government Printing Office, 1969

Kissinger, Henry, The White House Years, Little Brown 1979

Link, Arthur S., Woodrow Wilson and the Progressive Era, Harper Torchbook, 1954

Mowry, George E. The Era of Theodore Roosevelt, Harper Torchbook, 1958

Power and the Presidency, Robert A., Wilson, ed, Public Affairs, 1999

Rubel, David, Mr. President: The Human Side of America's Chief Executives,
    Time/Life, 1998

Russell, Francis, The Shadow of Blooming Grove, McGraw-Hill, 1968

Schlesinger, Arthur, Jr., The Age of Jackson, Mentor, 1955

Schlesinger, Arthur Jr., The Imperial Presidency, Houghton Mifflin, 1973

The American Presidency, Grolier (Grolier.com)

The Presidents, WhiteHouse.gov

Truman, Harry, 1945: Years of Decision, Memoirs of (Vol. I) New American Library, 1955

Truman, Harry, 1946-1952: Years of Trial and Hope, Memoirs of (Vol. 2) New American
Library, 1956

Wilson, Robert A., editor, Power and the Presidency, Public Affairs, 1999

Woodward, Bob, Carl Bernstein, The Final Days, Simon and Schuster, 1976

Woodward, W.E., Meet General Grant, Fawcett, 1957

US Presidents: Lists and Records www.heptune.com

Oneida County
Historical Society

The Oneida County Historical Society is member-based non-profit historical society conducting critical research, publishing engaging historical publications, retailing thousands of book titles and holding over 100 programs annually. The Colonel Tharratt Best Research Library serves genealogical and historical researchers. The Society's Your History Place Museum has wonderful changing exhibits.

The Society holds teacher workshops, historical tours and special events for members and the public.

The Society publishes newsletters, program brochures and other materials made available free to members. Membership and publication information can be obtained by contacting the Society at (315) 735-3642, ochs@midyork.org or 1608 Genesee Street, Utica, NY 13502.

The Oneida County Historical is a private 501 non-profit dedicated to serving the public. It is operated by three full-time employees and dozens of hard working volunteers. Official Mission Statement: "the Society's mission is to preserve the past of Oneida County and Central NY for present and future generations. The Society seeks to make this rich heritage readily available to researchers, families and students enhancing the Community's knowledge as well as appreciation of its history."

The Society was founded in 1875. It established the Oriskany Battlefield Monument in 1884, led the preservation of General Herkimer's Home which has preserved the rich history of the area and led the County celebration of the national Bicentennial.

Today the Society provides changing and engaging exhibits seen by thousands of visitors, area students and teachers. The Society also provides a research library serving thousands of researchers doing genealogy work as well as studying topics including Oneida County and Utica businesses, politics, music, architecture, religious and other topics. Collections on these topics include 250,000 documents and books, 45,000 photos, 30,000 three dimensional objects as well as slides, maps and also an extensive collection of local works of art.

TO: R. Ben Benson —

with admiration —

Barbara Bush

George Bush